CONTENTS

PLEASE GOD SAVE US

ART BY DEREK HESS : TEXT BY KENT SMITH

ART BY DEREK HESS
TEXT BY KENT SMITH

PRODUCTION BY VICTORIA SEMARJIAN
LAYOUT AND DESIGN BY ALISON GARTNER
EDITED BY KAIT STUEBNER AND ANNIE PEEBLES

PLEASE GOD SAVE US
First Edition 2008

Published in the United States by Strhess Press
1300 West 78th St Cleveland, OH 44102

ISBN 978-0-615-21242-5

www. strhesspress.com www.derekhess.com www.kentsmith.org

ACKNOWLEDGEMENTS

DEREK THANKS

My parents Roy & Joy Hess, Martin Geramita, Kent Smith, Metal Kait Stuebner, Victoria Semarjian, Annie Peebles, Alison Gartner, Chuck Crehore, Jakprints, Don & Jo Ann Geramita, Brett Bryan, Geoff May, Jon Timko, Kiki, Jose, Barack Obama, Al Gore, Michael Moore, Charles Darwin, Jimmy Carter, Steven Hawkins, Bill Clinton, Michael J Fox, Gerald Ford, Dennis Kucinich, Tim Russert, Bill Maher, Keith Olbermann, ZEITGEISTMOVIE.COM, Polar Bears, Cleveland Museum of Natural History, EVOLVEFISH.COM, Captain America, Black Sabbath, AC/DC, Iron Maiden and SpongeBob.

DEREK'S INSPIRATIONAL THANKS

The Republican Party, the hard Christian Right, the fossil fuel industry, Osterhus Publishing Company, Dial-the-Truth Ministries, The Fox News Network, creationism, intolerance, End-Timers, The Moral Majority, John McCain, Ann Coulter, Mike Huckabee, and religious extremists everywhere... God bless you.

KENT THANKS

I would like to acknowledge and thank the efforts of several individuals without whom, this book would not have come together. First of all, to Derek Hess for his willingness to enter the public debate in a powerful and original way with this body of artwork. Also, the other members of the Hess team, which is led by Marty Geramita and assisted ably by Kait Stuebner. Thanks and recognition needs to be conveyed to Davina Gutierrez, Dr. Jennifer Tserng and Emily Weglian for their issue specific expertise and suggestions. Special recognition and thanks are owed to Holly Klingler and Annie Peebles who served as content and style editors for the entire project. They read and re-read the book more than anyone and their input and editorial suggestions (and constant encouragement) were necessary and are greatly appreciated.

KENT'S INSPIRATIONAL THANKS

A deep and grateful thank you goes to the six who provided the foundation for all that I have ever written. They interceded in this young writer's career and provided inspiration to continue the craft. This book is dedicated to them: Pam Hooley, Audrey Chapman, Cindy Barber, Scott Lax, Lisa Chamberlain and Judy Smith.

Photo credit: Karen Novak

THIS BOOK HAS BEEN JOSÉ APPROVED

ABOUT THE NIGHT

THERE HAVE BEEN OTHER DEREK HESS ART OPENINGS IN CLEVELAND BEFORE. INDEED THERE HAVE BEEN DEREK HESS ART OPENINGS ACROSS THE GLOBE BEFORE. BUT HESS FANS HAD NEVER SEEN ANYTHING LIKE THIS. DEREK HESS GREW FROM AN ART STUDENT WHO DOUBLED AS A PART-TIME, UNDERGROUND CONCERT PROMOTER TO AN ARTIST WHOSE WORKS NOW HANG IN THE LOUVRE AND THE ROCK AND ROLL HALL OF FAME. CLEVELAND, OHIO IS HOME FOR HESS AND CLEVELAND'S 1300 GALLERY WAS HIS LOCAL HOST AND SHOWPLACE. ON DECEMBER 15, 2006, DEREK HESS' ***PLEASE GOD SAVE US FROM YOUR FOLLOWERS*** SHOW WOULD BE THE LAST ARTWORK TO HANG ON THE 1300 WALLS AS CLEVELAND'S MOST WELL-KNOWN, CUTTING EDGE GALLERY WOULD END ITS SIX YEAR RUN. IT WAS BOTH A FUNERAL AND A CELEBRATION. MORE THAN 500 ART LOVERS (SOME WHO CAME AS FAR AS TEXAS) GATHERED TO PAY TRIBUTE TO THE GALLERY AND ITS MOST WELL-KNOWN FEATURED ARTIST. WHAT THEY WITNESSED WAS ORIGINAL HESS ARTWORK WITH A NEW TWIST. IT WAS "HESS STYLE" BUT WITH A CHANGE IN FOCUS. THE COMPOSITION OF THE ARTWORK STILL FEATURED ATYPICAL PERSPECTIVES OF ANATOMICAL ILLUSTRATIONS. THE SUBJECT MATTER WAS STILL EMOTIVE, INTROSPECTIVE AND SPIRITUAL IN NATURE. BUT, THE EVENTS WERE CURRENT, THE SUBJECTS WERE MODERN, THE VILLAINS WERE REAL AND THEREFORE THE MEANING WAS OBVIOUS. SEE, HESS HAD GONE POLITICAL. BEFORE THAT NIGHT, HESS HAD ADDRESSED MODERN TIMES AND CULTURE THROUGH GENERALIZED ARTISTIC STATEMENTS AND WORKS. BUT, HE HAD NEVER FOCUSED ON ACTUAL INDIVIDUALS AND SPECIFIC EVENTS. ON DECEMBER 15, 2006, HESS DELIVERED A POINTED REBUKE DESIGNED TO ANGER AND INSPIRE. THIS BOOK NOT ONLY WILL ATTEMPT TO CAPTURE AND MEMORIALIZE THE NIGHT, BUT ALSO TO COMMUNICATE (IN WORDS) THE INSPIRATION BEHIND THE IMAGES. WE HOPE THE ARTWORK, AND ACCOMPANYING TEXT, WILL CONTINUE TO INSPIRE. JUST LIKE IT DID ON A SINGLE FRIDAY NIGHT IN 2006.

INTRODUCTION

DEREK HESS

I have never considered myself a political artist. Over the years I've been asked by people in Europe, "Why don't you draw politically charged art?" (In my opinion Europeans tend to have a better grasp on what's going on in America than Americans.) One of my reasons at the time was that I didn't want to "date" my artwork with a specific figure or event.

Over the past eight years, however, things have gone from bad to worse. When W won (or stole) his second election for the presidency, my feelings of helplessness were almost overwhelming. For the first time in my life, I seriously considered moving to another country. The only real thing I could do to resist was to use my pen. Not with words, but with images. This would, of course, date the body of work, but this fight is too important to not document.

As I began creating Republican based art, I started to put together all of the other things that helped Republicans occupy the White House. The hard-right Christian fringe groups, a certain TV network, and the fossil fuel industry, among other things. This enabled other groups to push their beliefs onto people who were perfectly happy with their own faith and ideas and knowledge of separation of church and state. The big picture was clear, many "agendas" were in play and were able to flourish during the past eight years.

This is why a portion of my work is now based on the themes of this book. Many pieces were generated before Kent came on board, but we are of like mind on these subjects and I feel both the artwork and text combined paint a clear picture of our stance on the state of the nation.

KENT SMITH

The purpose of this publication is to memorialize and explain the artwork of Derek Hess as it was displayed on December 15, 2006. The Hess opening was entitled *Please God Save Us from Your Followers* and it was the final art opening ever held at Cleveland's 1300 Gallery.

The art show contained over 40 original works by Derek Hess and it centered on a variety of religious, political and contemporary themes. Unlike Hess' prior works, which were more universal and timeless, this collection was urgent in its subject matter. Since it was a "one-night-only" show of originals, these 40 works will never be seen together again, except in this book.

The original collection has been joined by newer images created since the December 15th opening. The inspiration to explore these topics has continued beyond the 1300 opening because the problems they examine have not ceased to exist. Indeed, in some cases, inspiration has become more focused, more poignant, more dramatic, more tragic, more hopeful, more hopeless or some a combination of all six.

The message in the artwork will be discussed in the hopes that the images and words will create debate and provoke thought. But be warned—this book and this artwork is opinionated, controversial, compelling, provocative, sometimes sarcastic and sometimes funny. Neither the art nor the words claim to be fair and balanced; just factual and correct. Hess's goal of the art-opening was to challenge the complacent and the undecided; this publication takes it a step further—we want you to be convinced.

How you, the reader, chooses to react to these themes and topics is an individual choice. It is our hope—both artist and writer—that apathy will not be your endpoint. You may be angry, you may be motivated. We just ask that whatever the outcome; that you channel those emotions for good as you see it.

Be creative in your action plan; the world has ample ways it can be improved. Each of us knows what we can do to help. To those of you already engaged within the struggle, let this book strengthen and encourage you. Derek and I offer you our profound thanks and gratitude. And to those who will seek deeper meanings, further knowledge and a more just reality as a result of this work, we say make haste, be brave and enjoy your journey.

CHRISTIAN MESSAGE

HAS THE CHRISTIAN MESSAGE BEEN HIJACKED?

If there was an event that provided the inspiration to this collection of artwork it was witnessed by God and Derek Hess alone. While engaging in a typical morning, which included walking José (Hess' dog), and retail visits for incidental items, Derek Hess found a small 2-inch square Christian tract. On the front side of the tract, "Smile! God Loves You!" was written with a yellow smiley face. The flip side carried a slightly less positive message as it read, "But if you reject His love, given at great sacrifice at calvary, it would have been better for you not to have been born." Six New Testament Bible verses followed designed to provide comfort or panic.

The Evangelistic tract dropper and Hess had similar morning routines, and while they never encountered one another, they would trade propaganda. Hess would drop art house opening flyers, the unknown Evangelist would deposit Christian tracts. As Hess and José would walk, the tracts evolved into a body of work that examined modern American life, the Christian message and the Religious Right. Many of the following works incorporate the actual tracts that Hess found each morning.

THE CHRISTIAN MESSAGE IN AMERICA

America has a sin problem and God knows it. But it also has a unique Christian church when compared to the rest of Christian history. The American Church is both wealthy and free. In that respect it is unlike much of the church's past. In the 2,000 year history of Christianity, its system of beliefs was often illegal. There was no opportunity to develop a mega-church, it was all believers could do to assemble. Followers of Christ developed an underground language to stay alive which included the Jesus fish. Now a symbol on the backs of cars for proud public display, it was initially a secret password that allowed believers to find fellowship in a dangerous world. A world where their faith could cost them their life.

In modern America, believers do not to die for their faith. In the past, the Christians versus the Lions were seen as weekend football games. Perhaps in the wealth and safety of this country's religion, the command to love first has been replaced by the impulse to judge first.

While the American Church may be unique in its freedom, the power of the message remains. Many thousands, even millions, working through the process of daily recovery, acknowledge their dependency on a higher power. It is perhaps here, in humble recovery, where God remains active in a church controlled by wealth. Before Jesus died for the sins of America and the world, he was a humble carpenter. That carpenter can still restore souls and rebuild lives, but those miracles appear far away from television lights and sound bites.

The Church seems to work best for both Christian and non-Christians when it is a hospital for sinners and not a museum for saints. Christian fellowship was never meant to be as judgmental as high school. Perhaps the judgmental and materialistic have hijacked the message of Christ.

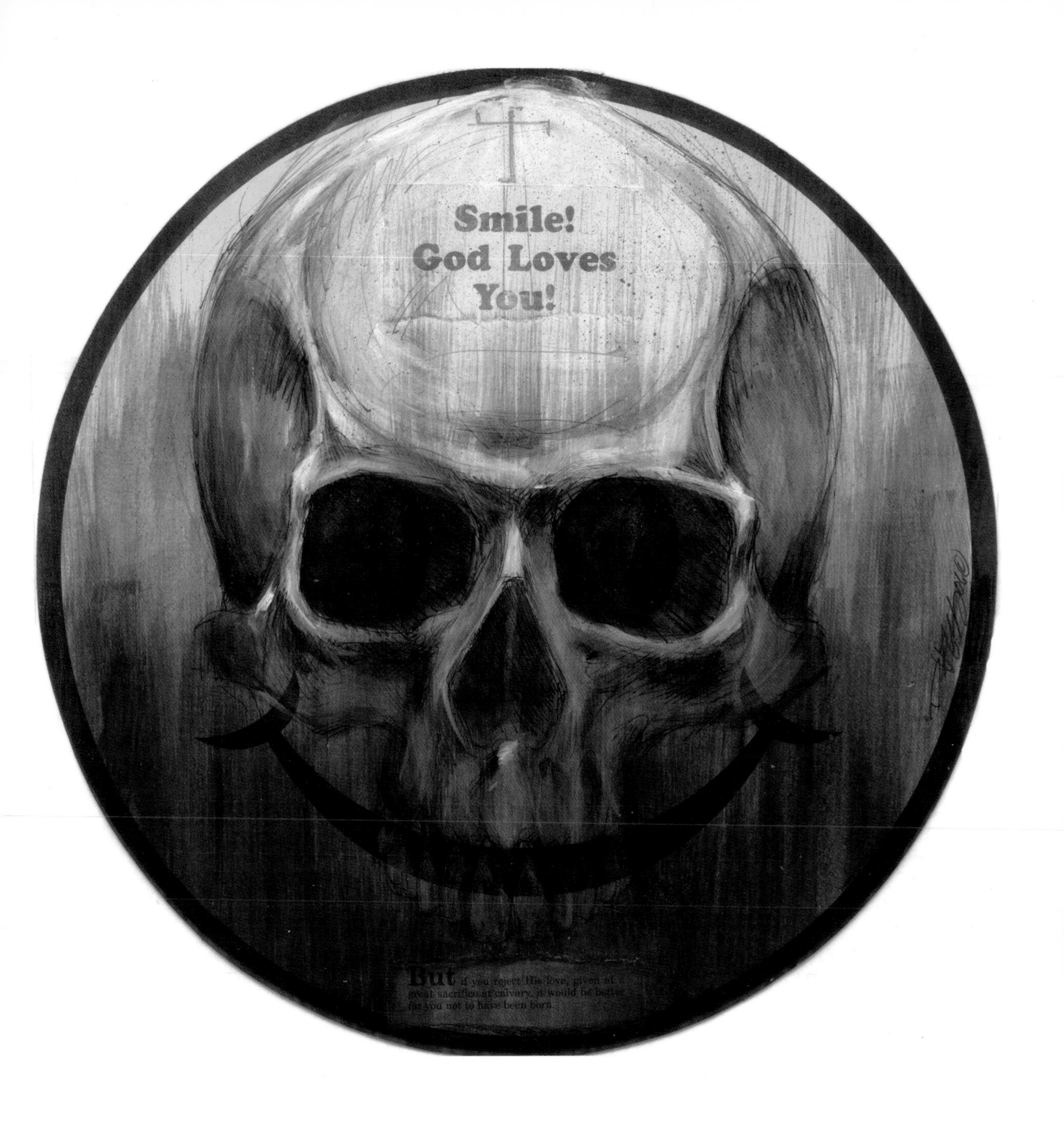

Smile

pen, ink, acrylic, torn flyer, on cardboard smiley face from a party store

2006

Most of the pieces in this group are inspired by "Smile God Loves You" flyers that I've incorporated into the art. What I found to be so inspirational is not the message on the front of the fliers, but the statement on the back. It reads, "BUT if you reject His love, given at a great sacrifice at calvary, it would be better for you not to have been born." When people see these fliers around they tend to think "fanatics" and get on with their lives. That's a problem. The less friction the producers of the flyers get, the bolder they will become, and those flyers are pretty bold as is. So this body of work is my attempt to wake people up to the enemy within.

The "Smile God Loves You" flyers are printed and distributed by Osterhus Pub House out of Minneapolis. www.osterhuspub.com

Pro-life Unless...
pen, ink, acrylic, 2007

Untitled
pen, ink, acrylic, 2007

Smile!
God Loves
You!

But if you reject His love, given at a great sacrifice at calvary, it would be better for you not to have been born.

Untitled
pen, ink, acrylic
2007

"JESUS ANSWERED THEM, 'IT IS NOT THE HEALTHY WHO NEED A DOCTOR, BUT THE SICK. I HAVE NOT COME TO CALL THE RIGHTEOUS, BUT SINNERS TO REPENTANCE.'" –LUKE 5:31-32

The freedom and wealth of the American Church has also led to the segregation of believers by race. While Jesus died for all mankind, the Jew and the Greek, the free and the slave, rarely will you find difference and diversity among the believers in the pews. Instead of using Christ's love to bridge the gap between the differences, the American Church has become a place where stereotypes are allowed to thrive. The Church has become another location for blasphemous lies of integration to create division. If Christ died for all, then why can't we live next to each other? If Jesus loves all, then why is Sunday morning in America the most segregated hour of the week?

In Romans 12:1–8, the Apostle Paul encourages the young Christian Church in Rome to be strong in their faith. Although they are facing difficult circumstances, he urges them to not abandon their God, their faith or their fellow Christian brothers and sisters. The beginning of the second verse reads as follows, "Do not conform any longer to the pattern of this world." Paul hopes they will understand this to mean—Be Brave! The American Church interprets it as an excuse to create segregated Christian communities. Don't believe me? How about this example:

About 35 miles Southeast of Nashville is Rutherford County, Tennessee, home of the proposed theme park called Bible Park USA. Bible Park USA is a Christian theme park which will sprawl out over 100 acres and cost between $150 and $200 million dollars. It will feature Biblical scenes from the Old and New Testament including Jesus' crucifixion. This will surely sell briskly in the gift shop.

How far we have come, American Church? You were lion food and soon you will have your own amusement park. By the way, Bible Park USA will be the second Christian theme park. But it will kick the ass of the first one, the tiny (only 15 acre) Holy Land Experience in Orlando, Florida.

THE RISE OF THE RELIGIOUS RIGHT—HOW IT HAPPENED

"DO TO OTHERS AS YOU WOULD HAVE THEM DO TO YOU. IF YOU LOVE THOSE WHO LOVE YOU, WHAT CREDIT IS THAT TO YOU? EVEN 'SINNERS' LOVE THOSE WHO LOVE THEM. AND IF YOU DO GOOD TO THOSE WHO ARE GOOD TO YOU, WHAT CREDIT IS THAT TO YOU? EVEN 'SINNERS' DO THAT." –THE WORDS OF JESUS, TAKEN FROM LUKE 6:31–33

How did the Christian message become the property of the Republican legislative agenda? Recent history illustrates that both major political parties have attempted to win on the moral highroad. In the television age, the first party to win the moral debate was the Democrats. It was the John Kennedy-led Democratic Party in the early 60's that led the nation with a moral message. Kennedy, and Johnson after him, proposed a Great Society, a war on poverty and a free land for all Americans regardless of skin color. As a Reverend became the point person for the civil rights movement, it was the Democratic White House that supported the cause. Kennedy's legacy, the Civil Rights Act, survived an 83-day filibuster in the United States Senate and was approved in the Summer of 1964. While Bible verses were quoted by both sides, the moral message was claimed and won by Democratic Party.

The Congressional and Presidential elections of 1964 provided a national validation of the Civil Rights movement pushed by the Kennedy and Johnson White House and the Supreme Court. By the way, Lyndon Johnson's Republican opponent in the 1964 elections was Arizona Senator Barry Goldwater. While in the Senate, Goldwater voted against the Civil Rights Act helping to make the Democratic moral argument stick.

The Republican Party found itself on the wrong side of the civil rights debate and they needed to craft a moral message that would restore their church member credibility. The Republican reaction to losing the moral highroad to the Democrats during the 1960's was to create fables of fear. These arguments were first seen when the Richard Nixon campaign suggested that these new reforms enacted by Congress and the Supreme Court went too far. New legal rights like having a government-sponsored lawyer provided to the indigent if they were so poor that they could not provide one or police no longer being able to force a defendant to testify against himself (they could not beat a confession out of the accused), were painted by Nixon as being soft on crime. The central strategy was to play on the decades of fear that were used to create the Jim Crow—separate but equal laws. While discrimination may have finally been outlawed, Nixon knew that racism was still prevalent.

The Republicans and Richard Nixon did not call it the "fear and distrust fables and lies;" instead terms like "family values" and "Moral Majority" were created with the goal to divide. The civil rights that Republicans sought to defend were vanilla and homogenous. Equal rights were embraced by the Republican Party just as long as you looked like them; and those who sat next to them on Sunday—then "rights for you" were fine. One of the founding fathers' reasons for writing the Constitution was to 'secure the Blessings of Liberty to ourselves', and as long as ourselves means "our people"—not the whole nation—everything was cool.

Execution Style
pen, ink, acrylic, torn flyers, 2007

Untitled
pen, ink, acrylic, flyer
2007

Untitled
pen, ink, acrylic, flyer
2006

THE MISSING MESSAGE OF THE RELIGIOUS RIGHT

"WATCH OUT FOR FALSE PROPHETS. THEY COME TO YOU IN SHEEP'S CLOTHING, BUT INWARDLY THEY ARE FEROCIOUS WOLVES. BY THEIR FRUIT YOU WILL RECOGNIZE THEM. DO PEOPLE PICK GRAPES FROM THORN BUSHES, OR FIGS FROM THISTLES? LIKEWISE EVERY GOOD TREE BEARS GOOD FRUIT, BUT A BAD TREE BEARS BAD FRUIT. A GOOD TREE CANNOT BEAR BAD FRUIT, AND A BAD TREE CANNOT BEAR GOOD FRUIT. EVERY TREE THAT DOES NOT BEAR GOOD FRUIT IS CUT DOWN AND THROWN INTO THE FIRE. THUS, BY THEIR FRUIT YOU WILL RECOGNIZE THEM." –JESUS, MATTHEW 7:15-20

PAUL WRITES TO THE CHRISTIAN CHURCH IN GALATIA, "THE SPIRIT, HOWEVER, PRODUCES IN HUMAN LIFE FRUITS SUCH AS THESE: LOVE, JOY, PEACE, PATIENCE, KINDNESS, GENEROSITY, FIDELITY, TOLERANCE AND SELF-CONTROL—AND NO LAW EXISTS AGAINST ANY OF THEM." –GALATIANS 5:22-23

The Republican Party leadership seem to believe the Bible only speaks to abortion and gay rights. Where is the emphasis on assisting the down trodden? Where is the command to help the poor? Where is the command to heal the sick? If Jesus said the second greatest commandment was to love your neighbor as yourself do you think he only meant if the family next door lived in a McMansion? While these may be Christ's commands, they somehow got left out of the Republican platform. Where is the sin of omission—in the Bible or the Republican political agenda?

How can a Party that claims to campaign with a divine message leave out such central themes in the Christian gospel? American poet, Ralph Waldo Emerson wrote, "Religion is to do right. It is to love, it is to serve, it is to think, it is to be humble." Perhaps the Religious Right should read more Emerson instead of pretending to have read the Bible.

Ronald Reagan was held up as the ideal President by many who support the Religious Right. This is the same President who advocated the substantial cuts to the social network to offset tax cuts for the wealthy. Reagan's argument was embodied in the "welfare queen" image. The "welfare queen" was a racial symbol used to push a stereotype that claimed the destitute were lazy and poor by their own choice. The "welfare queen" fictional persona was used to argue that the penniless had too much money.

Where is the compassion of Christ in the Religious Right? It is wrong to turn a blind eye to the downtrodden. Isn't that the central lesson of the Good Samaritan parable?

The "just get a job" argument only works when jobs pay more than minimum wage. When a 40 hour a week, minimum wage paycheck still leaves you below the poverty line, there is a problem. Where is the morality in an economic system that continues to suppress a class of people?

The Republican Party has used its pro-church message to divide the country and win elections. But they are not interested in making America a more Christian nation, in fact, they do not even believe the message themselves. If they let the Gospels shape their political agendas, they would not seek tax cuts for the wealthy at the expense of social programs. Their true colors are not just seen in their cuts to the poor, but also on the very issues that they claim to champion (like tax cuts for the wealthy). As Irish playwright George Bernard Shaw said, "A government that robs Peter to pay Paul can always depend on the support of Paul."

Perhaps a quote taken from *The Wall Street Journal* (9/9/2005) from one of their own is more damning. Congressman Richard Baker, Republican from Louisiana, in speaking to a group of lobbyists about Hurricane Katrina said, "We finally cleaned up public housing in New Orleans. We couldn't do it, but God did."

Christianity has become a weapon for submission and manipulation in the hands of men rather than a shield of kindness and compassion for all. It has become partial, divisive, and tyrannical. It no longer resembles the message of Christ, but another creature all together, and an ugly one at that. But all too often, it is the faux Christianity, the manmade political weapon it has become, that has caused others to deny God.

THE ABORTION EXAMPLE

Abortion has been the epicenter of the Religious Right. Some of what they have stated has been, "The unborn were always worth saving and protecting." "God's heart breaks when a fetus dies." "Vote for us and we will remove this curse from our nation; a nation founded on God's principles."

The Republican Party doesn't believe it and is not going to stop it. Consider the following:

If Roe vs. Wade was created by the US Supreme Court, then it can be undone by that same court. The current make-up of the court has already demonstrated its Republican leanings. When the US Supreme Court ended the Florida recount in Bush vs. Gore in 2000, it was clear that the balance of the court was Republican. But Sandra Day O'Connor was the swing vote that would maintain a woman's right to choose. However, O'Connor is now gone and the Court has the votes to make abortion illegal.

Yet, not only has the court not ruled on it—it has not even considered it. Let's face it: the American Church, the Republican Party and the Religious Right are only interested in furthering a set of economic policies that will concentrate and protect their wealth. Unborn life is a tool to get a segment of votes from a population that will not benefit from their "the rich first" programs and priorities.

If Roe vs. Wade were to be overturned, then law enforcement would have to investigate miscarriages as potential murder cases. Can you imagine how that would look on the evening news? That would mobilize a large segment of the female population, and Republicans would get thrown out of office in record numbers. Republicans will not allow Roe vs. Wade to be overturned because the political costs are too high. But they will continue to provide lip service to the pro-life position because it furthers their political agenda.

Christian fellowship that seeks God's will should leave the poor in better shape not make their lives worse. The greed of the Religious Right and the Republican Party have hijacked the Christian Message in America.

THE CLINTON HYPOCRISY

Bill Clinton's road to the White House hit a few speed bumps on the way—his infidelities. It came to light in front of a national TV audience when after the 1992 Super Bowl, *60 Minutes* let Bill and Hillary explain the other woman—Gennifer Flowers. Sadly, this would not be the last time President Clinton's indiscretions would take the national spotlight.

When President Clinton lied about Monica under oath, the Republicans pounced. Yes, he had lied about sex, but why was he being impeached—lying or sex? They said that Slick Willie had became a national embarrassment and an unfit leader of the nation due to his immoral personal life. The Christian Right had a new way to demonstrate their virtues and an impeachment would keep it in the papers for months. If they could not bring down Clinton, they could certainly make it hard for Gore.

Was Clinton wrong to lie under oath—yes. Did these affairs make Clinton a bad husband—yes. So he was being impeached for being unfaithful, right? Well, no—you can't get impeached for that. He was impeached for lying under oath. Did lying about sex mean that Clinton could not lead the country—no—and even the Republicans leading the charge knew it. Because they had all been bad husbands too.

The impeachment was about sex—even though that was not the charge. The Religious Right used the charges to rally their base and bash the sitting President. But the hypocrisy of the right wing moral venom was the Republican leadership could see the speck in Clinton's eye, but they could not escape the plank which hindered their own vision. Or maybe it was just that they could recognize a cheating husband because so many of them were cheaters too.

- Newt Gingrich admitted in 2007 to having an affair with a congressional staffer while the Clinton impeachment was proceeding. He would leave Congress in 1998.
- After Gingrich departed, the man who was chosen to replace Gingrich as the Republican Speaker of the House, Bob Livingstone, resigned from Congress when it was revealed he had also had an extra-marital affair. Livingstone resigned during the impeachment proceedings.
- Henry Hyde, Republican Congressman from Illinois who served as the lead Republican prosecutor against Clinton during the Senate trial was also forced to admit to an affair.
- The Texas Congressman who was then serving as the Republican Whip and would later become the Majority Leader, Tom DeLay (who would resign Congress after being indicted on money laundering charges), also acknowledged his own extramarital affair.

Don't Be So Mean

pen, ink, acrylic, flyer

2008

Untitled

pen, ink, acrylic, burned flyers and foam core in the shape of a cross

2006

THE REPUBLICANS FAILED THE SEX TEST

OK, maybe the impeachment was not about sex, but about lying. On July 3, 2007, W commuted the prison sentence of Scooter Libby, the former Chief of Staff of Vice President Dick Cheney. The Libby case is complicated, but it came down to this—when someone (Ambassador Joseph Wilson) pointed out how wrong W and Dick were about the Iraq War, the Bush White House set out to discredit and intimidate the Wilsons. Libby either revealed the identity of one of our country's intelligence officers (Wilson's wife) or he covered up for someone else's act of treason.

Regardless of how it happened, Libby was found guilty of lying to investigators about the breach of national security. But Bush commuted the prison portion of his sentence. So, Libby agreed to take the fall with the promise from Dick and W that he would never go to jail. Do you think he would have kept silent about who ordered what and who did what if he believed that he was being set up and might have to do hard time behind bars?

So the question has to be asked—what do Republicans hate more, sex or lying? Because they failed the lie test too.

The epilogue of the story is that Clinton lied, but, he finished his Presidency. None of the four Republican impeachment leaders (who were equally guilty of infidelity) remain in Congress today. I know it is not a Christian saying (so the Religious Right may not understand), but ain't Karma a bitch?

MORE FORGETTABLE REPUBLICAN EXAMPLES OF CHRISTIAN BEHAVIOR

Remember our friend and expert in adultery and money laundering, Congressman Tom Delay? When DeLay was asked how he approached the arrest process which included his mug shot photo he said, "I said a little prayer before I actually did the fingerprint thing, and the picture. And my prayer was basically: 'Let people see Christ through me. And let me smile.'" Certainly, Jesus has dealt with bigger problems than Tom DeLay—but you gotta wonder if Jesus was hoping to be left out of DeLay's booking photo.

Then there is Ralph Reed. He was the very public head of the Christian Coalition in the 1990's, and is a current Republican strategist. The White House visitation records (which are kept by the Secret Service) indicated that Reed had 18 meetings inside the White House between 2001 and mid 2006. He was a loyal Christian and a loyal Republican. This was a guy who had access.

A June 2006 bipartisan Senate report documented that Reed received more than $5.3 million dollars in payments from law breaking lobbyist Jack Abramoff. What would be worth over $5 million to a lobbyist who pled guilty to conspiring to corrupt public officials? Loyal church folk of course. Reed used his contacts among conservative Christian groups to drum up opposition to gambling interests who were the economic competitors of Abramoff's clients. It was Christian morality and indignation for hire. Again, I am sure Jesus is very appreciative.

"NO ONE CAN SERVE TWO MASTERS. HE IS BOUND TO HATE ONE AND LOVE THE OTHER, OR SUPPORT ONE AND DESPISE THE OTHER. YOU CANNOT SERVE GOD AND THE POWER OF MONEY AT THE SAME TIME." **–JESUS, MATTHEW 6:2**

BACK TO THE SIXTIES—JFK'S FAITH AND HISTORY REVERSED

One of the most interesting subplots to the Democratic moral victories of the 1960's was that they were led by a President (JFK) whose faith was questioned. When John F. Kennedy was the Democratic candidate for President in 1960, his Catholic faith became a campaign issue. Since America had never elected a Catholic to serve as its Commander in Chief, the suspicions swirled about JFK's true loyalties and possible hidden agendas.

On September 12, 1960, John Kennedy attempted to dispel these rumors through an address to the Greater Houston Ministerial Association. Kennedy managed to defend the first amendment and its guarantee of religious freedom while not disavowing his own faith. Among the highlights from his remarks were:

"WAR, HUNGER AND IGNORANCE AND DESPAIR KNOW NO RELIGIOUS BARRIERS."

"IT IS APPARENTLY NECESSARY FOR ME TO STATE AGAIN—NOT WHAT KIND OF CHURCH I BELIEVE IN, FOR THAT SHOULD BE IMPORTANT ONLY TO ME—BUT WHAT KIND OF AMERICA I BELIEVE IN."

"[THE PRESIDENCY] MUST NEITHER BE HUMBLED BY MAKING IT THE INSTRUMENT OF ANY ONE RELIGIOUS GROUP NOR TARNISHED BY ARBITRARILY WITHHOLDING ITS OCCUPANCY FROM THE MEMBERS OF ANY ONE RELIGIOUS GROUP. I BELIEVE IN A PRESIDENT WHOSE RELIGIOUS VIEWS ARE HIS OWN PRIVATE AFFAIR, NEITHER IMPOSED BY HIM UPON THE NATION NOR IMPOSED BY THE NATION UPON HIM AS A CONDITION TO HOLDING THAT OFFICE."

Kennedy's remarks stand in stark contrast to those who today hold the same office. Kennedy's example of tolerance provided him the vehicle to win the moral argument because he was trusted by all citizens—regardless of creed. With that trust in place, JFK was able to further America's agenda, not the Vatican's.

Kennedy's message of religious tolerance and freedom was also championed by Evangelical Christians who understood that Christ's message did not need the stamp of government approval. After all, if several hundred years of persecutions had not washed away Christian belief, why would a "backed by Congress and the White House" label really be needed? In 1986, during the height of Reagan's popularity, Carl F.H. Henry, the founder and former editor of *Christianity Today* wrote, "The church is not to use the mechanisms of government to legally impose upon society at large her theological commitments." Christian fellowship is not something the rest of the world should fear. And quite frankly, George Bush is giving Jesus a bad name.

Untitled
pen, ink, acrylic, torn flyers
2006

On this piece, I drew the figure first, with pen, ink, and acrylic. I then mounted it to a long rectangular piece of paper painted red that extended from the right and left sides. Once that was finished, I painted and tore two flyers and mounted them on top of the red on each side. This way the red showing through torn flyers creates a feeling of something menacing behind the message. I feel that if I had painted red on top of the fliers instead, it wouldn't have been nearly as effective.

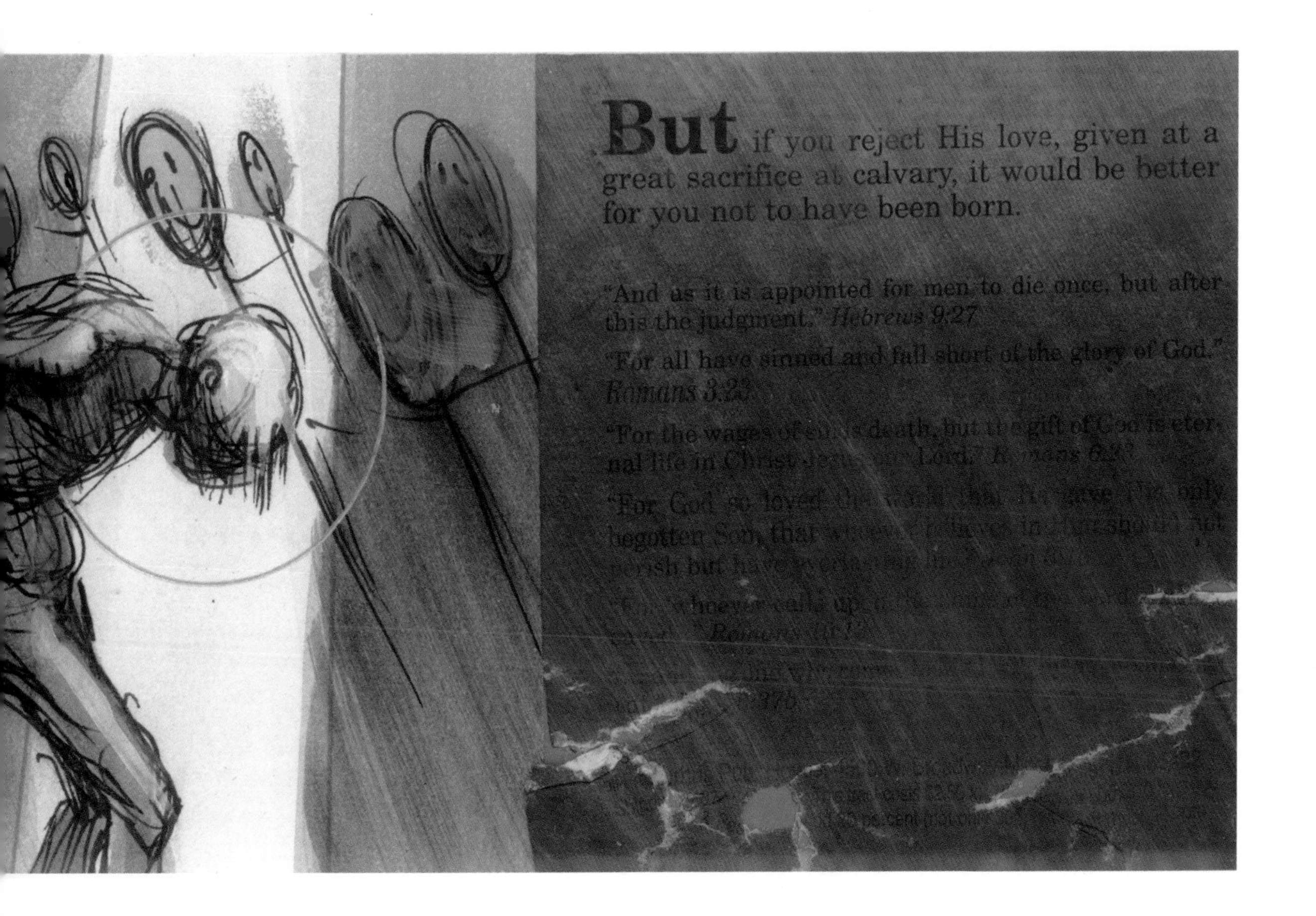

'HE SHINES HIS GRACE ON EVERYONE'

He Shines His Grace Down On Everyone
pen, ink, acrylic, flyers, mounted on board
2006

THE RED ELEPHANT GOES TO WAR

"NATURALLY THE COMMON PEOPLE DON'T WANT WAR; NEITHER IN RUSSIA, NOR IN ENGLAND, NOR IN AMERICA, NOR IN GERMANY. THAT IS UNDERSTOOD. BUT AFTER ALL, IT IS THE LEADERS OF THE COUNTRY WHO DETERMINE POLICY, AND IT IS ALWAYS A SIMPLE MATTER TO DRAG PEOPLE ALONG, WHETHER IT IS A DEMOCRACY, OR A FASCIST DICTATORSHIP, OR A PARLIAMENT, OR A COMMUNIST DICTATORSHIP. VOICE OR NO VOICE, THE PEOPLE CAN ALWAYS BE BROUGHT TO THE BIDDING OF THE LEADERS. THAT IS EASY. ALL YOU HAVE TO DO IS TO TELL THEM THAT THEY ARE BEING ATTACKED, AND DENOUNCE THE PACIFISTS FOR LACK OF PATRIOTISM AND EXPOSING THE COUNTRY TO DANGER. IT WORKS THE SAME IN ANY COUNTRY." **–HERMANN GOERING, COMMANDER OF THE LUFTWAFFE, GERMANY'S AIR FORCE DURING WWII**

"THE WORLD IS MY COUNTRY, ALL MANKIND ARE MY BRETHREN, AND TO DO GOOD IS MY RELIGION." **–THOMAS PAINE**
You can bet Paine would not have been hired by the Bush administration.

The Iraq War is about facts and fiction. The reasons for engagement were fiction. The facts are the costs, damages, profits and casualties. Christian fellowship is not something the rest of the world should fear. Yet this most Christian nation developed a war plan based upon fallacies and outdated information. In doing so, it damaged itself and the world.

HANS BLIX WAS RIGHT

Leading up to our ill conceived invasion, there were a few who knew the facts that attempted to provide a warning. But the rush to war was great and the truth would not get in the way. 9/11 provided the excuse and greed fueled the motivation. The bloodlust of misplaced revenge (not a very Christian motivation) was stoked by those whose stock portfolios would benefit.

As the cry for war grew loud and angry, it steam rolled dissent. Remember, Hans Blix and the UN weapons inspectors argued that Iraq was free of weapons of mass destruction (WMDs). Blix was the former head of the International Atomic Energy Agency who was called out of retirement by the United Nations in 2000. His task was to find out if Iraq harbored WMDs. With his background, he knew what to look for and he knew what could be hidden. In the beginning of 2003, Blix reported to the UN that Iraq most likely had neither WMDs nor the ability to produce them.

Blix was called a fool and a tool. Newt Gingrich said Blix was, "determined to buy time and find excuses for Saddam Hussein." The invasion began on March 20, 2003. Blix did not back away from his claims and soon others would support his statements, even members of the American government. In January 2004, David Kay, the lead US Arms Inspector said, "We were almost all wrong," when talking about Saddam's weapons programs. Bush did not agree. In October 2004, the person who replaced Kay, Charles Duelfer, issued a 1,000 page report that stated he found no evidence that Iraq produced any WMDs after 1991. Bush said but they would have if sanctions were lifted.

In 2005, the United States acknowledged that Blix, Kay and Duelfer were right—Iraq had no WMDs. And in June 2007, the UN Security Council voted 14-0 to shut down the unit which was charged with inspecting Iraq for WMDs.

...And That's Why Elephants Are Red
pen, ink, acrylic, comic book clipping
2006

Image inspired by Mark Motherbaugh's cover art for Henry Rollins book, *Pissing In The Gene Pool*

Jihad II
pen, ink, acrylic, comic book clipping
2006

Untitled
pen, ink, acrylic, comic book clipping
2007

AMERICA'S VOICES AND AMERICA'S BELIEFS

Bush said this war was because Iraq had WMD's. No weapons were found. Bush then said Saddam had strong links to Al Qaeda. No links were found. Bush then said that this war was necessary to defeat the terrorists. In 2007, a State Department study concluded that terrorists had increased 25% in the past year.

Bush's lies could not change the facts, but he could change the beliefs. The beliefs of the American people.

"IF YOU TELL A LIE BIG ENOUGH AND KEEP REPEATING IT, PEOPLE WILL EVENTUALLY COME TO BELIEVE IT. THE LIE CAN BE MAINTAINED ONLY FOR SUCH TIME AS THE STATE CAN SHIELD THE PEOPLE FROM THE POLITICAL, ECONOMIC AND/OR MILITARY CONSEQUENCES OF THE LIE. IT THUS BECOMES VITALLY IMPORTANT FOR THE STATE TO USE ALL ITS POWERS TO REPRESS DISSENT, FOR THE TRUTH IS THE MORTAL ENEMY OF THE LIE, AND THUS BY EXTENSION, THE TRUTH IS THE GREATEST ENEMY OF THE STATE." **–JOSEPH GOEBBELS, MINISTER FOR PUBLIC ENLIGHTENMENT AND PROPAGANDA FOR GERMANY'S NAZI PARTY**

Over and over again, Bush made his case to the American people. It did not matter that the facts did not support the war or the reasons for the war. A Harris Poll conducted between July 5–11, 2006 found that 50% of Americans believed that Iraq had weapons of mass destruction. Sixty-four percent of the Americans surveyed believed that Saddam Hussein had strong links to Al Qaeda. Goebbels would have been proud of this President.

The march to war required unwavering team loyalty inside the Bush White House. With the departure of Paul O'Neill and Richard Clarke in the winter before the invasion, groupthink went unchallenged in the Executive Branch. Still recovering from the wounds of 9/11, it was hard to argue for peace while the President was preparing for war. There were few American voices who fought the lies. Joseph Wilson, Former Ambassador to Iraq, attempted to stand up to the Bush falsehoods and the White House committed treason against his wife.

But those who cried "Wait" before the first bomb was dropped, before a single missile was fired, before any lives were lost were proved correct. Iraq was a country that was not a threat. And even this nation figured it out. Now a majority of Americans not only disapprove of the war, but more than half believe it is not even morally justified.

W COULD HAVE LISTENED TO DADDY

Maybe W didn't trust Hans Blix because he was from the UN and not Texas. Well, he could have listened to his father, George H. W. Bush, about some of the problems that awaited the American military in Iraq. By the way, Daddy was both from the UN AND Texas; he served as the US Ambassador to the UN from 1971–1973.

In 1990, Iraq invaded Kuwait, and then President Bush assembled a coalition of nations in a joint military venture to repel Iraq. After pushing Iraq out of Kuwait, the Gulf War forces had a choice, push North into Baghdad and overthrow Hussein, or not. Bush and members of his cabinet argued AGAINST the invasion. Among them was then Secretary of Defense, Dick Cheney. Cheney said invading Iraq would turn into a "quagmire" for American forces. Bush later justified his decision to not invade by saying it would have led to "incurred incalculable human and political costs...we would have been forced to occupy Baghdad and, in effect, rule Iraq." Daddy was right in 1991 and he is right now, and even Cheney agreed. However, this time, the Bush Cheney Rumsfeld Wolfowitz co-conspirators told America that Iraqi oil profits would finance the war. At most this war would cost us $50 to $60 billion. They also said WMDs would be found, American forces would be welcomed as liberators, and we could secure the peace with a relatively small amount of American troops.

OVERCOMPENSATION

THE BIGGEST LIE—THE WAR IS OVER AND WE WON

The invasion began in March of 2003. On May 1, 2003, President George Bush stood proudly on the deck of the USS Abraham Lincoln aircraft carrier which was docked in San Diego. The President spoke in grand language about the efforts of the coalition. Saddam Hussein's government had been removed from power and was on the run. He announced that major combat operations were over and that we had prevailed. Seen by TV cameras and the world, over the Presidents right shoulder, was a banner that read "Mission Accomplished."

Four years after that speech, President Bush would appoint a War Czar Lt. General Douglas Lute. Why would you need a War Czar if the mission was accomplished? At the time of Bush's speech, fewer than 150 military personal had lost their lives due to that conflict. Over 3,850 American military have lost their lives in Iraq since the speech. Why would more have to die if the mission was accomplished? Unfortunately, the last life lost has yet to occur.

This war has lasted more than five years. This war is now longer than the Civil War, World War I, and World War II. When this war started LeBron James was the best basketball player in Ohio—but he was still playing for his high school team.

The Bush White House was wildly and tragically off in every assumption. They were either willfully lying about the potential outcomes or they (with a clean conscience) were responsible for some of the most grave set of miscalculations in American history. The National Priorities Project says the current bill for this invasion is over $500 billion dollars. Nobel Prize-winning economist, Joseph Stiglitz from Columbia University, believes the overall cost of the war will reach $3 trillion.

The American Friends Service Committee estimates the cost of the war at $720 million dollars a day. That amount (based upon their calculations) is equal to the cost of providing health insurance for one year to 163,525 people. The daily cost of the war is equal to what it would cost to build 84 brand new elementary schools. The daily cost of the war could put 12,478 new teachers in classrooms. The daily cost of the war could fully cover the 4-year college tuition for 34,904 university students. The daily cost of the war could build 6,482 homes.

It cost $720 million dollars a day for a war that should not have been fought, created new enemies and our children will be paying off it for decades.

"I THINK THEY'RE IN THE LAST THROES, IF YOU WILL, OF THE INSURGENCY." **–VICE PRESIDENT DICK CHENEY, ON THE IRAQ INSURGENCY, JUNE 20, 2005**

Overcompensation
pen, ink, acrylic
2006

THE COST TO US AND THE COST TO THEM

If you re-read Thomas Paine's quote at the beginning of this chapter, you could argue that the "us and them" should be seen as "we." The tragic reality is that more American lives have been lost due to the Iraqi War than were taken from us on September 11, 2001. On the sixth anniversary of 9/11, 789 more American lives have ended in Iraq than were lost in New York City, Washington DC and a Pennsylvania field. The current American military death toll is over 4,000. All for an untruthful war. America's war wounded totals between 30,000 and 53,000. All for an invented and unnecessary military invasion. Linda Bilmes, a Harvard economist estimates that the lifetime health care tab for the wounded troops will be between $250 and $650 billion dollars.

As dangerous as Iraq has been for American soldiers, the war has been much more deadly for Iraqi civilians. Perhaps as an indication of the degree of chaos on the ground, the estimates of civilian deaths vary widely. At the end of 2006, the US—backed Iraqi government believed that 12,357 civilians had been killed whereas the United Nations' tally was much higher at 34,452.

The website, icasualties.org estimates that as of July 2007, over 31,000 Iraqis have died as a result of the war. Ironically, the US Government keeps no such official statistic, but the Department of Defense has kept a rough average of casualties per day during different periods of the conflict. For example, from May 20, 2006 to August 11, 2006, the department said there were nearly 120 Iraqi casualties each day.

"THERE IS NO FLAG LARGE ENOUGH TO COVER THE SHAME OF KILLING INNOCENT PEOPLE."
–**HOWARD ZINN, AMERICAN HISTORIAN AND POLITICAL ACTIVIST**

According to the UN, the Iraq War has led to 1.2 million Iraqi refugees. The organization Refugees International believes the total to be more than twice that (2.5 million). These are innocents caught up in the crossfire and fleeing for their lives. They are willing to leave behind much of what they own in an attempt to escape the violence. Do you think these people appreciate our invasion? How are we viewed—as a benefit or a plague? Do they view us as liberators or murders? Do you think any of them might want to strike back at us sometime in the future? Is this a war to stop terrorism or an invasion which will plant the seeds of our future enemies?

But it is not just Iraq, pretty much everyone hates us now. A July 2007 study done by the Pew Research Council showed the world's attitude towards America has sunk like a Hummer in quicksand. Hostility is highest in three former allies—Turkey, France and Pakistan. When your former friends now hate you more than anyone else, what does that say about you?

Republichrist Jihad Devil
pen, ink, acrylic, 2007

This image is inspired by 14th century depictions of the Devil. Some of these creatures had grotesque monstrous faces growing out of their stomachs and hind quarters. The Republichrist is leading the charge to war with a "Crosstika" staff (half swastika, half cross). It's designed to create blind faith and allegiance, much as the swastika was used by Nazi Germany.

REPUBLICHRIST JIHAD DEVIL

HALLIBURTON

So why did we do it? Why invade now when we didn't decades earlier? The most troubling answer is greed. It also might be the answer that is most correct.

The Iraq War accomplished many things—virtually all of them bad. This war does not make the world safer or our nation stronger. This war depletes our resources in every way imaginable. It does, however, feed the military industrial complex, and one company in particular (Halliburton) was a leading benefactor. Halliburton was formerly led by Vice President Dick Cheney until he stepped down to become George Bush's running mate. Surely, this is just a coincidence.

The value of Cheney's stock options rose from $241,498 in 2004 to over $8 million in 2005. When Congressional Democrats wanted to ask questions of the billions in war contracts that Halliburton received, the Republicans blocked it. FYI: It is reported that Halliburton has received upwards of $13 billion for this war and KBR (a Halliburton spin-off company) has war contracts that total $18 billion. Wait, why did we invade again?

As American military loses have increased, so has Halliburton's stock price. As Iraqi civilian loss of life has grown daily, Halliburton's profits continue to soar. As more countries leave the tiny coalition that entered Iraq with the United States, reliance upon US forces and US companies will continue to grow. And that will increase American war casualties and Dick Cheney's bank account. How many lives per gallon were lost? How much money was wasted to make our national interests less secure?

When Cheney was interviewed by ABC News' Martha Raddatz regarding the fifth anniversary of the war, she asked him his thoughts about recent polling "that show about two-thirds of Americans say the fight in Iraq is not worth it." Cheney's response? He said, "So?" It's worth it to Dick Cheney.

The epilogue to the Halliburton story—in March 2007, Halliburton announced it would open a new corporate headquarters in Dubai of the United Arab Emirates. Its current CEO would relocate from Houston to the new HQ in the Mid-East. To paraphrase the 1980's band The Call, "Dick Cheney is just a corporate criminal playing with tanks."

The Surge

pen, ink, acrylic, comic book clipping

2007

THE RED ELEPHANT AGENDA

MORE FOR ME

The true priority of Red Elephant agenda is not that America remains the home of the brave or the land of the free, but rather the haven for the wealthy. The Republican strategy is to divide the public on issues so their riches can be protected. Think of the debates that have emerged. They divide one race against another. They divide union workers against the environmentalists. They anger and isolate the church population against the huddled masses that God commanded them to serve. They attack dissenting opinion as non-patriotic. They engage in smoke and mirrors tactics to keep the focus off their main mission, protecting the concentration of wealth. Their wealth.

NOT FOR ALL THE PEOPLE—JUST OUR PEOPLE

This thinly veiled self-interest is seen in the Republican Party's social agenda and their economic platforms. Guess who they like more? The Party of Lincoln needs to re-read the final part of the famous phrase first heard at the Gettysburg Address in 1863; "of the people, by the people, for the people." Let's look at the attitudes of the Red Elephant concerning the social services safety net.

US Senator (D-Ohio) Sherrod Brown was exactly right when he said the strategy that Republicans employ on social policies was to "under-fund, criticize, and privatize." We will call this strategy the 'More for Me' plan. The Republican agenda is to keep as much of their money as possible. It is not to end poverty, heal the sick or ensure our elderly can live their golden years in respect and safety.

Republican Party leaders are not living in poverty, so they seek to cut food assistance programs. When they get sick, they get the best health care money can buy, so creating greater affordable access to health care is unnecessary. As their parents age and require more care and medical attention, they get it. However, the average family sees their meager savings accounts sucked dry by a health care system built on asset recovery not quality of life. The Red Elephant education goal is not to provide kids a world-class education or make college more affordable, they just want to get richer. There is no "for the people" emphasis in the Lincoln Party today.

"YOU WORK THREE JOBS? UNIQUELY AMERICAN, ISN'T IT? I MEAN, THAT IS FANTASTIC THAT YOU'RE DOING THAT." **–PRESIDENT BUSH, TO A DIVORCED MOTHER OF THREE IN OMAHA, NEBRASKA, FEBRUARY 4, 2005**

HOW IT IS SUPPOSED TO WORK?

There is a natural and healthy tension between Capitalism and Democracy. Capitalism is the survival of the fittest of the marketplace, Pepsi vs. Coke; Letterman vs. Leno; Sevendust vs. the Worst of American Idol; whatever. Democracy is the survival of the majority, such as Bush's win over Kerry in 2004 or Gore's win over Bush in 2000.

Capitalism and Democracy, both powerful forces, sometimes collide. Their conflict is fine; they need to balance each other out. Occasionally, the free market may overpower the common good. The marketplace is driven by stock market dividends. It does not see the harm its economic system can do; it only sees the green that its greed returns.

Democracy, however, needs to provide the balance to corporate ambition. It needs to develop forward thinking, future-minded policies to protect future and present generations from the dash for cash that can trample lives. Problems can arise when government does not have the backbone to stand up to the corporate interests because it has been bought off, or if the super wealthy control the government.

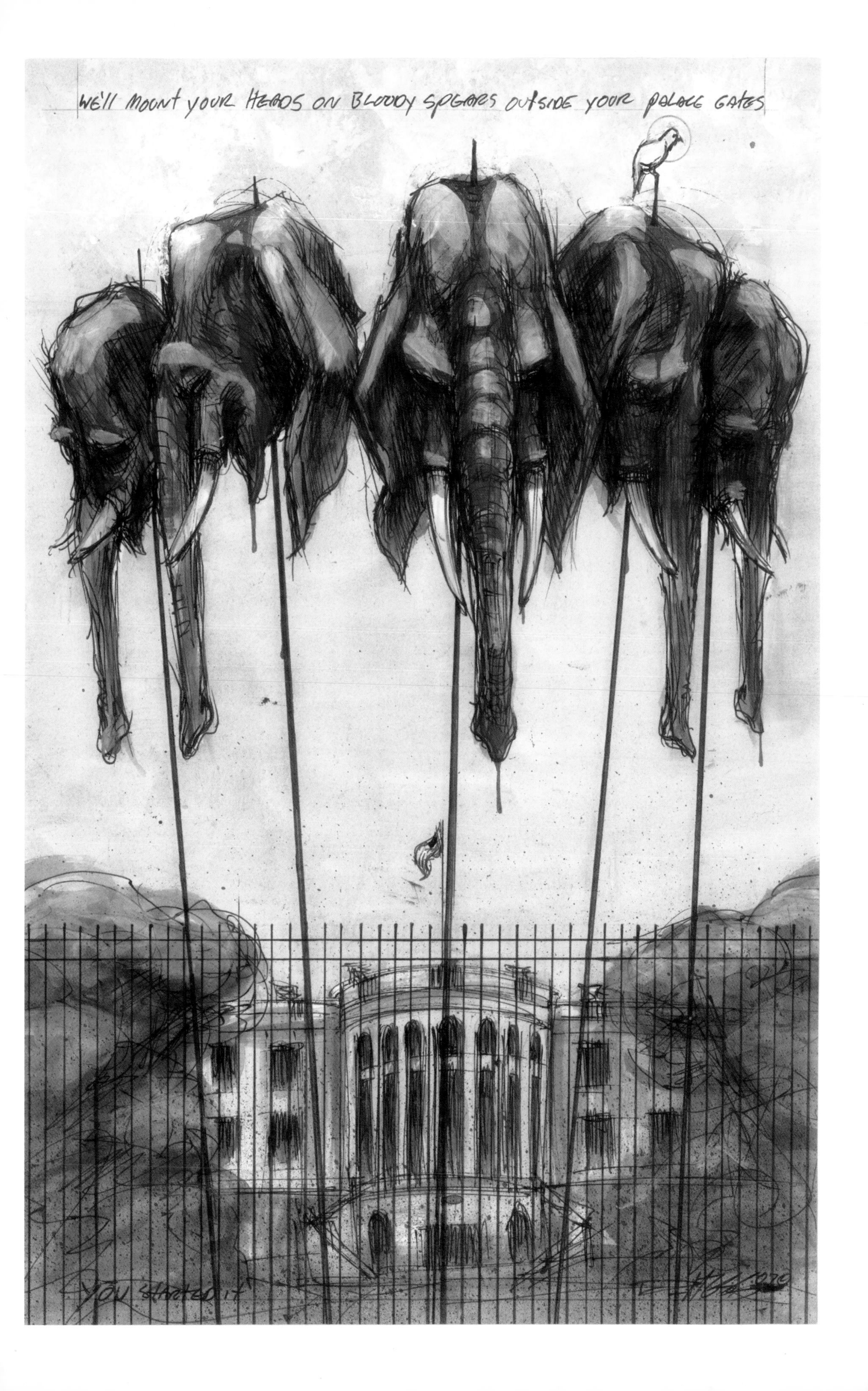
WE'LL MOUNT YOUR HEROS ON BLOODY SPEARS OUTSIDE YOUR PALACE GATES
YOU STARTED IT

You Started It (previous page)
pen, ink, acrylic
2007

The line across the top, "We'll mount your heads on bloody spears outside your palace gates," is by the band The Sword. Although these lyrics have nothing to do with this subject matter of this image, I thought they worked pretty well with this piece (and, I like The Sword a lot).

Crosstika
pen, ink, acrylic
2006

The Crosstika flag is raining, I mean reigning down on its subjects.

God Says No

2006

God has sent his angels down to Earth to put an end to the Republicans using His name for their bidding. In this piece, their bidding is trampling on the Constitution and pissing on everything this country was founded on.

Untitled
pen, ink, acrylic
2004

Republichrist
pen, ink, acrylic
2006

Again, the Crosstika is used in this image to illustrate a similar message as in *Republichrist Jihad Devil*. In this one, the elephant and Crosstika aren't leading the masses to war, they're re-enforcing the blind faith and allegiance through the manipulation of religion. The hands raised in praise are inspired from a scene in the movie *Jesus Camp*. In one segment, the children are taught to pray to a cardboard cut out of George W. Bush. Some of them are actually crying.

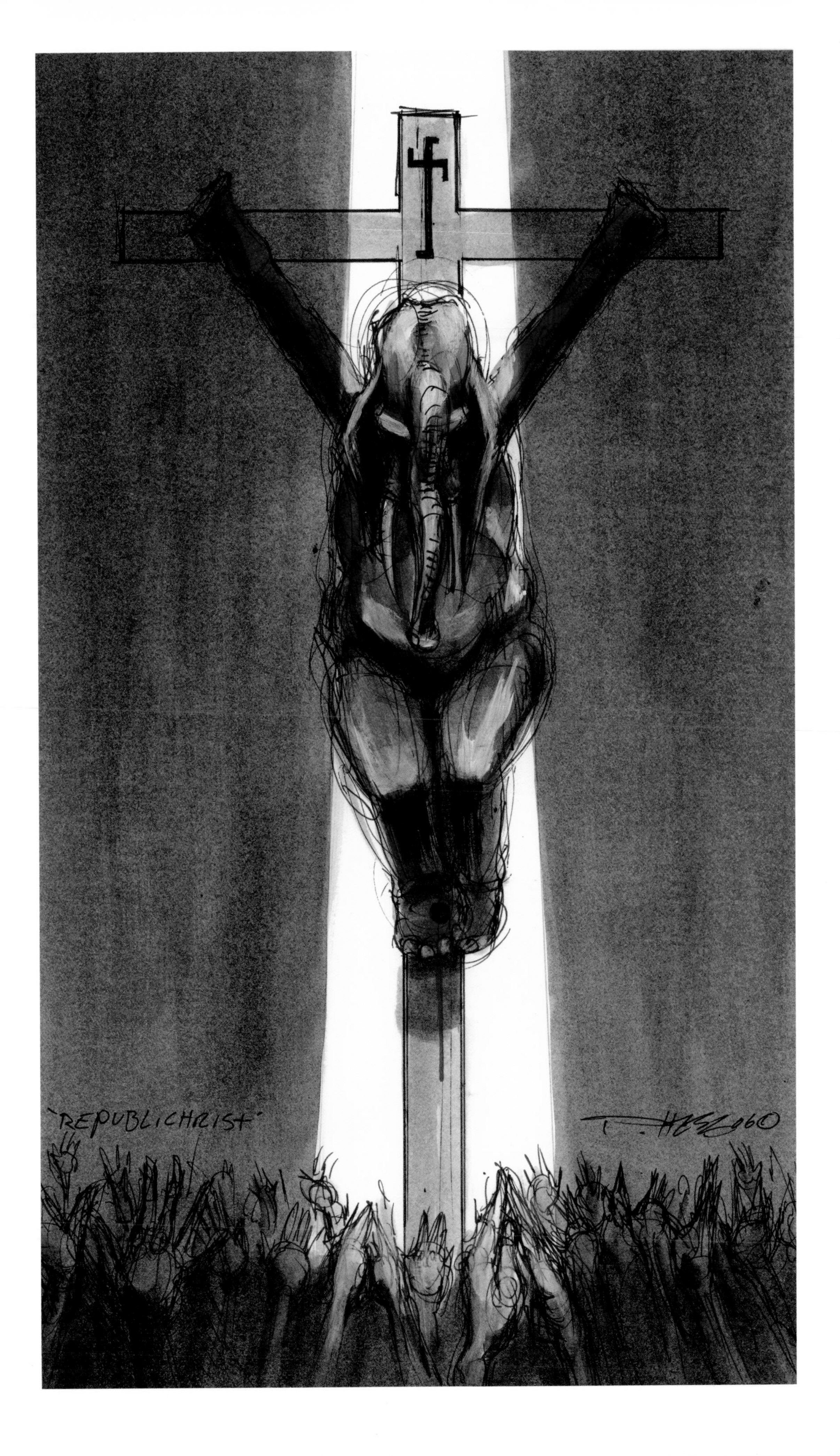
"REPUBLICHRIST"

THE MORE FOR ME TAX CUT

The federal government does not control the economy, but it can set forth economic policies that can help grow investments or wages. Growing investments help those who currently have money (usually the wealthy). Growing wages can help those who are living day to day, paycheck to paycheck. Guess what Bush did? In mid 2001, he cut taxes by $860 billion, $630 billion of which was targeted to the top 1% of income earners—whose average salary were 1.1 million dollars. Who do you think that helped? Well, in 2005 (the last year of available data), the top 1% of Americans made 21.8% of all the dollars earned in America. This was their largest share of the American pie since 1929.

Government by the rich and for the rich leads to a world that only the wealthy want to live in. Today's largest economic threat is that we are creating an economic system that has damaged the largest economic asset the country has—the middle class. The good news is the federal government understands the balance between Capitalism and Democracy. The bad news is the current President continues to craft policies that are designed to afflict the afflicted and comfort the comfortable.

Here is an example—let's divide up personal income into five parts. The top quintal is those individuals who are in the top 20% of income earners. The bottom quintal is the poorest 20%. In 1980, the top 20% earned 43.7% of all the national income. In 2004, that percentage had increased to 49%. That means the remaining 80% of us were earning less. The middle class is slipping and the comfortable are getting a bigger piece of the pie.

WHY IS THE MIDDLE CLASS IMPORTANT?

Because there are more of them. The middle class buys more cars than the wealthy buy stretch Hummer limousines. Personal consumption (middle class spending) generates 67% of all Gross Domestic Product. If you damage the economic standing of the middle class, in the end, you will hurt the entire economy.

Wages and salaries make up the lowest proportion of the economy since the US government began keeping track of those figures in 1947. Corporate profits are at their highest share since the 1960's. Ohio has lost 20% of its manufacturing jobs since Bush took office, which is a total of 195,000 formerly well-paying jobs. These were middle class jobs.

The spin on the Bush "More for Me" tax cuts was the assumption that it would jump-start the economy, and it did—for the rich. Further evidence the Bush tax cuts didn't work can be found in a study by the Economic Policy Institute (EPI). EPI built the case that the Bush tax cut did not lead to better economic standing for the nation. The study examines the current economic cycle to past averages of previous economic recoveries. In Gross Domestic Product, the Bush recovery was less. In payroll and jobs, the Bush recovery was less. In personal income, the Bush recovery was less. In consumption, the Bush recovery was less. This was not a tax cut—this was a stick-up.

OTHER FACTS AND FIGURES—MORE BAD NEWS

In the summer of 2007, the Democratic-led Congress finally raised the federal minimum wage which had not been increased since 1997. It ended the longest time without a raise since the minimum wage was first established in 1938. Adjusted for inflation, the minimum wage had not been this low in more than 50 years. Before the increase, a minimum wage worker earned only $10,700 a year. Why punish workers?

The formula that is used to determine the value of the Food Stamp program, which helps to feed over 25 million Americans, has not been adjusted since 1996. A third of these 25 million are children. Why punish poor kids? What would Jesus do? What should W do?

45 million Americans do not have health insurance. 54.5 million Americans did not have health insurance during some part of the year—that is 18.6% of the American population. The for-profit health care insurance industry is making us all sick. Last year more people declared bankruptcy than graduated from college.

"THINGS ARE GOOD FOR AMERICAN WORKERS." **–GEORGE BUSH, AUGUST 2006.**

Intervention pen, ink, acrylic, 2007

This piece could have been called "Divine Intervention" as well, but I feel the image gets the Divine point across by its self.

INTERVENTION

Thrown
pen, ink, acrylic
2006

23
pen, ink, acrylic
2006

In this piece, I wanted to make a statement on the true source of evil in contemporary times. So, I used the theme of Satan and the snake that tempted man in the Garden of Eden, but the red figure of evil in this one is an elephant.

THE RED ELEPHANT APPROACH TO GLOBAL WARMING

MORE SUNSCREEN & TURN UP THE A/C

In 1986, the Surgeon General released a study that would change the smoking debate forever. It was the first landmark study to conclude that secondhand smoke caused disease. The tobacco industry attempted to discredit the science of the report and fought the allegations with, smoke and mirrors. But that report was the beginning of the end. The tobacco industry would lose billions in forthcoming lawsuits and while smoking continued, no reasonable person would ever again believe that smoking was a harm-free behavior.

Fast forward more than 20 years and there is a new second hand smoke—but unlike tobacco, it is a cloud that we cannot escape. The potential for damage to personal health and our environment is growing as are the warnings.

The increase in greenhouse gases has created a landfill sized pile of credible studies and data suggesting that our present course will cause planetary adjustments that will lead to generations of hardships for the human race. Be clear about one thing—it will not lead to the destruction of the planet—the planet will survive without its most offending party. However, our fate will not be kind. We need to negotiate a new path that is healthier for our host ecosystem or risk the permanent eviction of our future generations.

The lack of national leadership on an international problem hurts our credibility as a global leader. In fact it makes us look selfish, greedy and stupid. But this is the standard procedure for the Bush administration and to be expected from two old men who made their fortunes in the oil industry.

The reality is the Red Elephant will struggle to survive as the global temperature rises. Burying one's trunk in the sand will not cool the earth. It will just make the Elephant more vulnerable to prey. The more recent strategy of denial replaced political deceit and election lies. During the 2000 campaign, Bush (running against environmental advocate Al Gore) pledged to impose mandatory limits on greenhouse gasses. He renounced this promise after his election.

Since the pachyderm is slow to acknowledge the threats, some of the evidence will be reviewed. We know that the elephant never forgets. We just hope this one is willing to learn.

Red Elephant vs. Polar Bear
pen, ink, acrylic, 2007

'RGO. ELEPHANT VS POLAR BEAR'

Untitled
pen, ink, acrylic
2006

Yellow Reign
pen, ink, acrylic
2007

CONSIDER THE FOLLOWING, ENDANGERED, OVER-SIZED, SUNBURNED PACHYDERM:

In 2005, the scientific journal, *Science,* reviewed all credible scientific articles published between 1993 and 2003 involving climate change. None of the articles disputed the theory that human behavior was contributing to the warming of our planet.

Do you want research that is more current? Okay, in early 2007 the Intergovernmental Panel on Climate Change (IPCC) released a report that concluded climate change was occurring as a result of the actions of man. The report stated that there was at least a 90% chance that human-caused emissions were the primary factors in the increase in global temperatures since 1950. The increased amounts of greenhouse gases were trapping heat inside earth's atmosphere and that was creating a variety of changes on the planet; changes that could create a bleak future for the third rock from the sun. Five of the potential outcomes:

- The Arctic Ocean could largely be devoid of sea ice by later in the century
- Mediterranean Europe might become so hot that it would be virtually uninhabitable
- Drought conditions are likely to expand in Africa and southern Asia
- Sea levels will rise therefore jeopardizing existing coast lines
- Mountain glaciers will melt at an escalating rate.

You may wonder just who is this IPPC? It is a panel created by the United Nations in 1988. You may also wonder just who wrote this report for the IPCC? A collection of 600 scientists wrote it. Then it was reviewed by another 600 scientists.

THE GREAT LAKES ARE TURNING INTO THE SHALLOW PUDDLES

In March 2007, a study by the American Geophysical Union published a study that Lake Superior (the largest of the fresh water great lakes) is rapidly warming. Based upon research that includes daily temperature readings from the past 102 years, the surface temperature of the lake has increased 4.5 degrees since 1979. The lake's "summer season" is now beginning about two weeks earlier than it did 27 years ago.

Professors at the University of Minnesota Duluth wrote a study which concluded that the jump in surface temperature was not only a symptom of climate change, but also a reinforcing factor. The water warming trend could mean less ice cover in the winter which would lead to more solar radiation and additional water loss resulting in exponential warming. This leads to the lake becoming shallow.

Lake Superior, like all the Great Lakes, is seeing its water level drop. As the water level decreases, it reduces the shipping lanes and large freighters cannot carry as much material inside them. If ships have less cargo, then their companies make less money.

The argument in response to this research is essentially this; a green planet is fine—if by green you mean money. We know that you can't be a capitalist and a tree hugger. If you want the standard of living to increase, you must accept the consequences. If the planet gets hotter, so what, it's capitalism that moves our lives forward, not clean air and water, right?

But it is not just in the Midwest that water issues are starting to boil. Two mountainous states, Wyoming and Montana, will have their water dispute settled before the United States Supreme Court. At issue is the water from the Tongue and Powder Rivers which run through both states. In 1950, the two states negotiated an agreement on water usage that Montana now maintains Wyoming has violated. What is not in dispute is that water has become scarcer in this part of the country that has experienced a prolonged drought since 1999. How valuable will water become if the drought continues? What could possibly be causing lower water levels and an extended drought?

GLOBAL WARMING—A PROBLEM FOR BUSINESSES AND ARMIES

But what if there was some research that concluded global warming was actually bad for business (aside from those cargo ship companies in the Great Lakes)? Could that change the debate? A British Government authored report was released in October 2006 stating climate change could impact the global economy similar to the Great Depression. The estimated cost to economies would be between 5% and 20% of the world's gross domestic product. In comparison, during the 1950's, American military spending averaged about 4% of our nation's gross domestic product.

One thing is certain, the longer the world waits, the larger the price tag. If the earth's nations chose to reduce greenhouse gases over a 50 year period, it would cost about 1% of global economic activity. In US dollars that is about $120 billion a year. $120 billion was the size of Bush's 2001 tax cut. It was roughly how much was spent on the Afghan and Iraqi wars in 2006.

Maybe a pro-business argument will help get the President moving.

On April 16, 2007, a 68 page report was released which was authored by 11 retired Admirals and Generals. The report was designed to look at the Climate Crisis from a national security perspective. The military men concluded that global temperature increase could create more worldwide conflicts. The escalation in temperature would endanger one billion people who live within 45 miles of the coast. The increase in drought conditions could lead to substantial drops in available food and water. This report arrives at the conclusion that taking steps to reverse global warming now may lead to less military treats and conflicts in the future.

Maybe a pro-national security argument will help get the President moving.

THE RED ELEPHANT RESPONSE TO GLOBAL WARMING—TWIST ARMS AND DENY

"CATASTROPHIC GLOBAL WARMING IS A HOAX." – **REPUBLICAN SENATOR JAMES INHOFE, JULY 28, 2003.**

Before the Democrats took over the Senate in 2006, James Inhofe was the Chairman of the Senate Committee on Environment and Public Works. During the 2002 election cycle (the last time he was on the ballot), only Texas Republican Senator John Cornyn received more campaign dollars from the oil and gas industries.

Nine out of ten warmest years on record have occurred since 1994. Resisting reality and demanding others to resist it also, does not change reality.

The 1997 Kyoto Protocol was the first agreement of substance on the threat of global warming. It became a symbol of global consensus on an emerging international threat. Bill Clinton signed it, but the Republican controlled US Senate refused to ratify the agreement. It has been signed by 141 other countries. However, the agreement does not include three major countries: the US, China, and India. The US continues to road block the Treaty while the world suffocates from our smog.

In January of 2006, *The New York Times* reported that the top climate scientist at NASA, James Hansen, was being pressured to stop speaking about the warming planet. Hansen was restricted from talking to the media and had to have his lectures, papers and web postings cleared by the NASA public affairs staff.

Perhaps Hansen was just bitter. Surely, the US Government would not prevent a scientist from sharing information about topics that could impact global health. Our "Christian" government would not do that, would they?

Well, they did it at least one other time. On March 9, 2007 *The New York Times* reported that two scientists from the Fish and Wildlife Service would not be allowed to speak about or answer questions at international meetings regarding various global warming topics. Polar Bears and sea ice and climate change were specifically off limits. The G-8 nations produce 40% of the greenhouse gases, the primary pollutant which results in global warming. The leading polluter in the world is the United States. Second and coming up fast is China. Instead of acknowledging our global responsibility, Bush often uses the "China Excuse" for the lack of US action on global warming. But this is an argument of convenience and laziness for what is yet another version of the "More for Me" plan. Personal greed takes precedent with this President over clean air, water, and land.

The US, while having only 5% of the earth's population, produces 25% of the emissions that cause global warming. If the US does not engage in a meaningful reduction of green house gases, China and India have no reason to do so either. And the global problem of manmade industrial second hand smoke will continue to grow.

Republicans Hate Polar Bears

pen, ink, acrylic

2006

Another end result of global warming and polar bears. I chose to use a "dumb" red elephant on this one.

THE RED ELEPHANT VS. THE POLAR BEAR

One of the Hess pieces depicts an elephant that resembles the Disney character Dumbo sitting on top of dead polar bears. It is sarcastically titled *God Hates Polar Bears.* FYI: We actually think God likes polar bears.

One of the unavoidable outcomes of the global warming problem is it affects all living things on the globe. Animals lives are dependent upon their natural surroundings and their long-standing food chain. According to a 2004 study, the Northern latitudes are warming twice as rapidly as the rest of the globe. Temperatures are predicted to rise an additional 13 degrees Fahrenheit by 2100. This could reduce the arctic ice cover by 50 to 100 percent. Researchers have determined that the ice on Canada's Hudson Bay is breaking up two and a half weeks earlier than it did 30 years ago. OK, but how does this affect polar bears?

Due to the warming Arctic, the polar bear finds its habitat is changing—and not for the better. Polar bears hunt during the summer when their primary food source, ringed seals, return to the Arctic. Polar bears, the largest bear on the planet, use the summer ice as hunting platforms as they search for food. After hunting from one ice platform, they dive in the water and swim to another patch of ice. But less sea ice means less hunting; less hunting means less food. If the food intake of polar bears is reduced then bears are thinner which decreases the reproductive rates of female polar bears. The survival rate of cubs has also decreased which has caused a 21% reduction in the polar bear population from 1997 to 2004.

But the lack of sea ice does not just mean polar bears are thinner. It also means some have drowned in the arctic since they have had to swim larger distances between ice patches. Scientists have also discovered evidence that polar bears have resorted to cannibalism to survive.

Environmental groups and scientist have noticed the increasingly tragic plight of the polar bear and have asked the US Government to consider adding them to the threatened species list. The Bush administration did what you would expect, they delayed. They studied the polar bears plight for two years. On December 15, 2005, three environmental groups filed suit against the government to speed up the polar bear evaluation.

You might wonder, what is the big deal? Just call the polar bears "threatened" and be done with it. Why would the government delay? Because if a listing of "threatened" is bestowed upon a species, a government is prohibited from doing anything that would further harm the animal or its habitat. And if global warming is creating the problem, then the endangered polar bear might force W to stop global warming.

Maybe in the future we can say thanks to polar bears.

On The Backs Of Polar Bears

pen, ink, acrylic, burned bottom edge

2007

OTHER GOVERNMENTS ARE TAKING STEPS—SO SHOULD THE US

Luckily, political will is a renewable resource. In other words, the failure of yesterday does not necessarily guarantee failure tomorrow. While W and China use each other as an excuse to protect their pollution profits, other governments are more willing to make difficult choices to protect our planet.

In May 2007, the mayors of some of the world's 15 largest cities including London, New York City, Chicago, Toronto, Tokyo, Sydney and Karachi agreed to an aggressive plan to reduce their city's greenhouse gas emissions. This partnership, based upon a carrot-and-stick approach, increased conservation and reduced energy use reducing global carbon emissions by 10%.

Also, in May of 2007, Japan pledged $2.1 billion to fight climate change.

Back here in America, two regional statewide partnerships (with the support of Republican governors) have been developed to reduce carbon emissions.

On May 31, 2007, George Bush went from a strategy of denial to delay regarding global warming. He suggested the G-8 nations develop a plan to curb greenhouse gases sometime during 2008. Much like the Iraq War, W is just messing it up; he will let the next President fix his disaster.

Mr. President, the time to act was years ago yet your administration engaged in systematic deception and intimidation. After lies on this topic and others, why should we believe you now?

GLOBAL WARMING LEADS TO POISON IVY AND LAWSUITS

Two recent studies (2007 University of Maryland & 2006 Duke) suggest that the increased amounts of carbon dioxide in the air leads to a stronger, bigger, and itchier poison ivy. Soon camping will be impossible because the wilderness will be paved over except for the man-eating crops of poison ivy.

As of December 2006, there were no fewer than 15 climate change lawsuits in the state and federal court system. Some of these were filed by state governments (California vs. six major auto makers) and some were filed by private attorneys (a class action of Hurricane Katrina victims vs. oil companies, utilities, and coal producers).

In February 2007, the CEO of Exxon Mobil, Rex Tillerson said, "We know our climate is changing, the average temperature of the earth is rising, and greenhouse-gas emissions are increasing." If the leader of the largest oil company in the world can recognize the problem of climate change, maybe we should do something? Unless you like poison ivy and lawsuits.

End-Timers
pen, ink, acrylic
2006

The End-Timers are an extremist Christian group that believes we are in "end times", which is to say Jesus will be coming around the mountain when he comes. Some of these End-Timers are elected officials in the Republican Party. The truly scary thing is that End-Timers believe if we can hurry up and deplete the Earth of its natural resources and destroy the environment, the sooner the second coming will arrive. This way, they can all go to heaven and the rest of us will have to live in the hell they created. This is another motive for our government not to protect the environment, and actually loosen up restrictions on pollution control, and drilling for oil.

red stacked elephant
pen, ink, acrylic
2008

Gasmask
pen, ink, acrylic
2007

THE RED ELEPHANT'S GOP STANDS FOR THE GREEDY OIL PARTY

It is impossible to ignore the same two men who are leading our military forces are also developing our nation's energy policy. These men made their fortunes in oil. They owe their wealth to black gold and America's increasing appetite for it. So, the question is, whose interests are Dick and George more concerned with, America's or the family's bottom line?

Across the globe, more than $4 trillion dollars is spent every year on "conventional" energy. America consumes 21 million barrels of oil a day, two-thirds of which is imported. Someone is getting rich, but who?

Fortune Magazine's top 20 most profitable companies of 2006 included three oil companies in the top ten. At number 8—ConocoPhillips, saw a 15% increase in their profits on the $15.5 billion that it earned. That year's number 7—Chevron, the second largest US oil company, made $17.1 billion; a 22% increase over its previous year. And the most profitable company in America for 2006—Exxon Mobile. It pulled in $39.5 billion, the biggest corporate profit amount in history. Whose record did it break? It's own from 2005, when Exxon only made $36.1 billion. In 2007, the profits continued to roll. Exxon broke its record just a year later—in 2007 it made $40.6 billion. We think we know who is getting rich.

THE PAIN AT THE PUMP

If gasoline prices go up, does the executive branch fret or smile? The prices of gasoline and natural gas have more than doubled since 2000. In January 2001, when two oil men took over the nation's capitol, the average price of a gallon of gas cost was $1.13 and a barrel of oil cost $32.21. In the summer of 2006, that same gallon of gas was up to $2.97—a 162 percent increase. In the spring of 2008, gasoline continued to set price records at $3.75 a gallon with US Energy Department predicting future price increases still forthcoming.

In 2006, that barrel of oil was just under $70 ($69.30)—a 115% increase from where it was in 2001. As a point of reference, the inflation rate during that period of time was 12.7%. Much of the inflationary increase was due to the amazing spike in energy costs. On January 2, 2008 a barrel of US light crude oil hit $100 for the first time in history. In March of 2008, the price of a barrel of oil set new high price records six times in seven trading days. Its peak price (which will soon be broken again) was $125 in May, 2008.

How much of the gas price increase is due to 9/11? Not much. In early February 2003, six weeks before the Iraqi invasion, the price at the pump was $1.75 a gallon. America spends $1.25 billion a day on gasoline. You know what happens when gas prices go up? Poor people cut back and rich people pay more—just the way those Red Elephants like it.

Acid Reign
pen, ink, acrylic
2006

Skeptics wondered if the dip in gasoline prices before the November 2006 elections would last. It did not. Gas prices hit all time highs about six months after the Republicans got tossed from power. Gas prices jumped more than 25% during the Spring of 2007 without a significant increase in the cost of crude oil. This increase in fuel costs forced consumers to pay more gas and less for everything else. Unfortunately, we all didn't get 25% raises. The springtime 2007 jump cost Americans an estimated $20 billion—which is about $146 for each car on our nation's roads. And those costs have continued to soar.

The spin we were handed was the lack of refineries which are needed to convert the oil to gasoline. The energy industry pointed to the fact that no new refineries had been built since 1976. What they left out was that existing refineries had been modernized and national capacity had actually increased 13% since 1997.

Global supply and demand is not working in favor of the US consumer. China currently imports three million to 3.5 million of barrels of oil a day—which is expected to increase 7% a year as its economy continues to grow. The point of this is; Yes, we might discover new oil reserves and yes the oil industry continues to press for additional exploration (including in the areas up north that used to be covered in ice), but any new additions to the global oil supply will likely only feed the growing Chinese demand. Oil is not renewable. This is not a problem we can drill our way out of.

Where (in the expert's eyes) are the largest untapped oil reserves? In order: Russia, Iraq, Kazakhstan, Canada, Saudi Arabia, Venezuela & Iran. At least Canada likes us.

MORE THAN CARS

However, energy is not just for cars, it is also for electricity in our homes. There are many different ways to solve the problem or to ignore the issue. Take appliances for example. Under W's "leadership" no appliances had been required to reduce their energy usage and become more efficient. In 2005, 15 states joined several environmental groups and sued the Department of Energy to review the energy standards for almost two dozen residential and commercial appliances. They claimed that current technology (if required by law) could save enough energy to meet the needs of 12 million American households. What purpose (aside from greed) does it serve to *not* increase efficiency when the technology is available and effective?

OK, so you don't want to buy a new more efficient refrigerator—can you change a light bulb? The lighting industry has developed a corkscrew-shaped fluorescent light bulb that uses 75% less electricity and last 10 times longer than the incandescent light bulb. Each bulb saves the customer $30 over the life of the bulb. If 100 million new bulbs replaced the old bulbs then customers could save $3 billion on their electric bill and the atmosphere would be saved from an additional 20 million metric tons of green house gasses. The three billion dollars in energy costs saved is equivalent to the energy needs of 450,000 new homes. So, start changing light bulbs.

WAS THE IRAQI WAR A SMART MOVE FOR US ENERGY POLICY?

According to the National Priorities Project, the US Government's Iraq War expenditure has surpassed $520 billion. Keep in mind—one of the reasons given for why we fight is energy independence. Dick and George are committed to protecting our Christian oil even if it happens to be under their Muslim sand. So after spending in excess of $500 billion has this nation been freed from it is oil addiction?

What else could be done with the money for Bush and Cheney's war? One option is it could have been used to buy 23.2 million Toyota Prius hybrid cars. There are an estimated 204 million vehicles in the nation. What would that do to energy prices and our global dependence on oil?

How much does the Prius save? If it averages 50 miles per gallon over 100,000 miles (as opposed to the non-hybrid 25 miles per gallon). That is 2,000 gallons of gas saved. Basic economic theory says if the demand for a product drops, the price of that item would also fall. What would 23.2 million hybrid cars do to our dependence on foreign oil if each auto saves 2,000 gallons of gas per vehicle?

Maybe you do not want a new car—consider yet another option. In the mid-1990's, the United Nations estimated that it would cost $40 billion per year to provide the basics of life—adequate food, clean water, health care, shelter, and literacy—for every person on the planet. That works out to $151 per American. Compare that to the cost of the war. Which expenditure frees us from our addiction to oil? Which expenditure puts money in our leader's pockets? Which expenditure would a true Christian nation seek first? What is a more Christian use of dollars?

IS SOMEONE HIDING THEIR GREED?

We know that gas prices went up 162% in the first six years of Bush's presidency. That increase is 10 times the level of inflation during the same period of time. You want more evidence that Dick and George are more concerned about oil profits than America? You want more evidence that the US Supreme Court is more concerned about Republican profits than the restoration of ethics and principles? How about this? In 2001, Dick Cheney met with various business leaders from the oil industry to develop our national energy policy. Which leaders did the Vice President meet with? Well, we don't know, he won't tell us.

Before the war, Democratic Party interest groups sued using the Freedom of Information Act to gain access to the federal energy policy deliberations that were being led by Vice President Cheney. In other words, Cheney was sued to force him to tell us which energy industry big wigs were helping to shape our national energy decisions. Truth does not need to be kept from public view, greed needs to be kept from the public view. Cheney would not share his list of industry allies so the case went to the Supreme Court. The US Supreme Court allowed Cheney's secret energy policy deliberations to remain hidden. This decision should cause us to be distrustful of the Court's loyalties and the administration's priorities.

Kennedy gained the trust of a skeptical nation by pledging to advance the standing of all America's citizens. Bush and Cheney have squandered their election mandate by continuing to seek policies that further themselves first—at the expense of the citizenry who put them in office.

DID THE 2006 ELECTIONS HELP ANYTHING?

Things got better after the Democratic gains in Congress as a result of the 2006 elections, right? Actually, no, not right away. Immediately after the election, the Greedy Oil Party knew they were being thrown out of power. So, the oil and gas companies got a lovely parting gift from the outgoing Republican majority. They were given wider access to oil and gas drilling in the Gulf of Mexico. No surprise considering the heavy PAC contributions that were provided to Republican members of Congress.

Things got a little better after the Democrats took over. In late June 2007, a new US energy policy bill passed the US Senate. The new bill included the first significant increase in automotive fuel standards since 1975. While he was in the Oval Office, President Clinton wanted to increase the fuel standards (called the CAFE standards), but the Republican Congress prevented it. One of the ways to hold pace with increasing demand is to increase efficiency at the same time. Increasing the miles per gallon requirement for automobiles does that.

However, the new energy bill could have been much better. The GOP was able to help defeat two important measures that need to be revisited in future days, for the good of the nation and the planet. First, a requirement that utility companies purchase 15% of their energy from renewable sources. This requirement would need to be met by 2020. Second, a $32 billion tax shift that would have raised taxes on oil and energy companies. Those revenues would have been earmarked for the research and development of alternative fuels.

So, let me get this straight, the government could tax the older sunset industries which pollute our earth and endanger our national interests to help develop new energy sources that will only grow in global market demand. While financing these emerging clean technologies, they could ensure a market demand by forcing power companies to use these renewable energy sources. But no, somehow that seems too logical. Let's just add more carbon to the skies, grow the profits of oil companies and increase the American body count in a war based upon lies.

Did we mention that electric utilities have given over $110 million dollars to federal campaigns and candidates since 2000? That figure ranks them in the top 25 for industry lobbying interests. Maybe that had something to do with this enlightened energy policy.

The goal should be to develop an energy policy that is renewable, natural, free and clean. If that goal is achieved, then the country would be safer and the world would be cleaner. The only losers might be the families who make their money fortunes in oil.

Untitled
pen, ink, acrylic
2006

Sketch of *Environmental Policy*, page 64

THE RENEWABLE ENERGY STRATEGY—HOW IT COULD WORK

The technology currently exists to turn wind, sun, corn, even garbage into energy. If only we could find some near by.

Wind Power: There are eight wind turbine manufacturers worldwide; only two of them (GE and Clipper) are American. The demand for turbines exceeds supply. The earliest delivery dates currently stand at 2009 and 2010. It is a $13 billion dollar a year industry currently dominated by the Europeans.

While the US only gets about 1% of its national energy needs from wind power and the industry is moving quick. It has grown on average 29% each year between 2000 and 2005. Anyone want to start a turbine company?

A wind power report came out of Northeast Ohio in November of 2006 that said that investing in wind energy could create 10,000 jobs. It also predicted that within ten years, wind power in Ohio could provide 10% of the state's energy need—which could power more than one million homes.

A labor coalition called the Apollo Alliance thinks that a 10-year, $300 billion research investment could create three million "green collar" jobs by 2017. Green collar meaning jobs in the renewable energy field.

But there is no demand, right? Actually FirstEnergy (HQed in Akron, Ohio) in December 2006, signed a 23 year agreement with a Scottish based company to buy 34.5 Megawatts from wind power for their customers. The Scottish company has not even built the wind farm yet, but the demand is in place. Interesting in part because in August 2006, First Energy set a new record for power demand by its customers. Again, anyone want to start a turbine company?

Solar Power: It works well on a variety of scales. Consider the following: the City of Cleveland is going to install solar panels on some of its fire stations and other municipal buildings. The solar heat will provide between 50% to 70% of the hot water needs for the fire station. Also in Cleveland, there are solar panels on the top of Progressive Field where the Cleveland Indians play. Perhaps this will add some pop to the Tribe's bats.

You may ask, what about cloudy days? Yes, the sun shines more in some places than it does other; but it shines enough everywhere to be an energy source. With the exception of VP President Cheney's cave, the sun shines everywhere. The US Energy Department operates the National Renewable Energy Library in Colorado. They estimate that Cleveland would receive approximately 75% of the sun of San Diego. Both climates have enough sun to help save the earth.

'ENVIROMENTAL POLICY'

But solar power is not just for fire stations any longer. Utility scale solar projects currently exist in Portugal, New Mexico and in the California Mojave desert. Similar large-scale solar parks are scheduled for Nevada, Australia and Canada. GE is one of the major investors in this technology and the company is hopeful that large, massive-scale, solar-powered utility projects could satisfy home and business energy needs in the not to distant future. No drilling, no pollution, no national security risks, just sunlight and mirrors and a way to capture that energy and send it off to the waiting consumer.

There are 31 companies that make solar panels in the US. First Solar LLC in the Toledo, OH area produces more than any other American company. Every one of those Solar panels goes to Germany where the government incentives are larger and more established. Anyone want to start a solar panel company?

Corn: It is from the Mid-West not the Mideast. In 2005, Ohio farmers produced 465 million bushels of corn. Each bushel of corn can produce 2.8 gallons of ethanol fuel. The most recent ethanol based fuel blend is a type of flex fuel called E85 which is 85% alcohol and 15% gasoline.

There are just under 100 ethanol plants nationwide. In the next five years, that number could double, and corn based fuel could increase from 4.3 billion gallons to 7.5 billion gallons of renewable, Mid-West grown fuel. Ethanol production needs to become more efficient and that is why we need more research. It would be better for this nation if we were importing our fuel from Iowa and not Iran.

Garbage: A Cleveland based company has developed a way to turn landfill gas into food grade carbon dioxide and high quality methane motor fuel. Currently millions of cubic feet of landfill gas are burned 24 hours a day wasting enough energy to power nearly every garbage truck in the country. What if they could run on fuel which was derived from the very rubbish they hauled the day before? Well, they could.

CAN GOOGLE SAVE THE EARTH?

Yes, *that* Google. They recently flipped the switch on a huge solar panel installation at their Mountain View, California headquarters. The sun powered source of natural energy will generate 1.6 megawatts. That is enough to power 1,000 average sized California homes. They also recently awarded a $1 million grant to develop a plug-in hybrid car capable of getting 70 to 100 miles per gallon. Perhaps this is part of the reason that Google is worth more than the big three US auto makers combined.

Environmental Policy
pen, ink, acrylic
2007

No clean energy source will get in the way of the Right's fossil fuel profits.

EVOLUTION

FUN WITH SKELETONS AND LAWS

All the elements for a good argument are included in the Creationism vs. Evolution debate: freedom of speech, freedom of religion, separation of church and state, public education policy, the politics of science. So let's first cover the critical milestones of the science.

Charles Darwin first published *On the Origin of Species by Means of Natural Selection, or the Preservation of Favoured Races in the Struggle of Life* in 1859. The major component of the work was the theory of natural selection which allowed species to adapt and survive over time.

In 1953, the research team of James Watson and Francis Crick published *A Structure for Deoxyribose Nucleic Acid* which identified the human genetic code. It became the road map for subsequent discoveries.

In 1973, Donald Johanson discovered the famous Lucy skeleton in Africa.

THOSE FUN TRIALS

Creationism and evolution have occasionally bumped legal heads. The most well-known case was a 1925 trial that took place in the Rhea County Courthouse in Dayton, Tennessee. This landmark case became known as the Scopes Trial because the defendant was a high school science teacher named John Scopes. Scopes was a 24-year old teacher who also served as the school's football coach who had been arrested for teaching the theory of evolution. Scopes became a criminal thanks to the Butler Act of 1925 passed by the Tennessee state legislature. The law banned the teaching of any world/human creation theory that was not supported Biblically.

The trial featured high profile attorneys that included Clarence Darrow for the defense and William Jennings Bryan for the prosecution. Bryan was a three time failed Presidential candidate who had served as the nation's Secretary of State. During the trial Darrow put Bryan himself on the stand. The trial was covered by journalists from over 200 newspapers across the globe and was the first trial to be broadcast on national radio. Scopes was found guilty and fined $100; his conviction would later be overturned. The trial was the inspiration for the play and movie *Inherit the Wind.*

Other states passed laws, and often those laws turned into courtroom cases, some of which have been appealed to the nation's highest court. The US Supreme Court has always sided with evolutionary science, saying that the creationist theories were the advancement of religious belief and did not have legitimate educational standing.

Supporters in the Creationistic doctrine repackaged their beliefs into what was called Intelligent Design Theory. Intelligent Design had its time in Federal Court in 2005. The Kitzmiller vs. Dover Area School District lawsuit questioned the academic merits of including the creation theory of Intelligent Design in the science classroom. The Dover School Board in Pennsylvania believed that Intelligent Design was a legitimate science which deserved instruction time in the Dover School District. It was a bench trial (no jury, the Judge would decide) presided over by John E. Jones III who had been appointed to the federal bench by W in 2002.

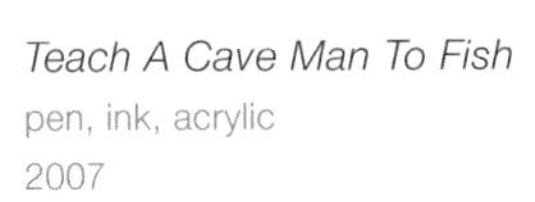

Teach A Cave Man To Fish
pen, ink, acrylic
2007

Cincinnati Fish Meets Cleveland Dunkleosteus–
The Battle Of Ohio
pen ink, acrylic
2007

I went to the Cleveland Natural History Museum and drew the fossil remains of Dunkleosteus Terrilli. I then put this 360 million year old fish skull on the Darwin evolution fish and have it taking a bite out of fiction.

FOSSIL REMAINS OF A 360 MILLION YEAR OLD FISH CALLED "DUNKLEOSTEUS TERRILLI" WERE FOUND IN THE SHALE ROCKY RIVER OHIO - IT NOW RESIDES IN THE CLEVELAND MUSEUM OF NATURAL HISTORY

OHIO

2010

DARWIN
A - MASTODONS WERE TOO BIG TO GO ON THE ARK - SO THEY DROWN
B - EXTINCT CREATURES WERE ON THE ARK, THEY DIED OUT LATER
C - FOSSILS NEVER WERE ANIMALS, THEY'RE A HOAX BY SATAN
D - FOSSILS NEVER WERE ANIMALS, THEY'RE A HOAX BY GOD TO TEST YOUR FAITH
E - NONE OF THE ABOVE

E, None Of The Above

pen, ink, acrylic, canvas, safety pins

2006

OK, there's a lot going on here…first off I drew the Mastodon skull at the Cleveland Natural History Museum like I did in *The Battle Of Ohio* piece. I made it red to illustrate the Republican elephant extinction, along with the Creationists who support them. The angel and devil fluttering around the Darwin fish represent fiction confronted by fact. The heavenly light is shining down onto the truth. Then truth being the answer to the multiple choice which is E., none of the above. I gave the Mastodon a gold tooth just for the hell of it.

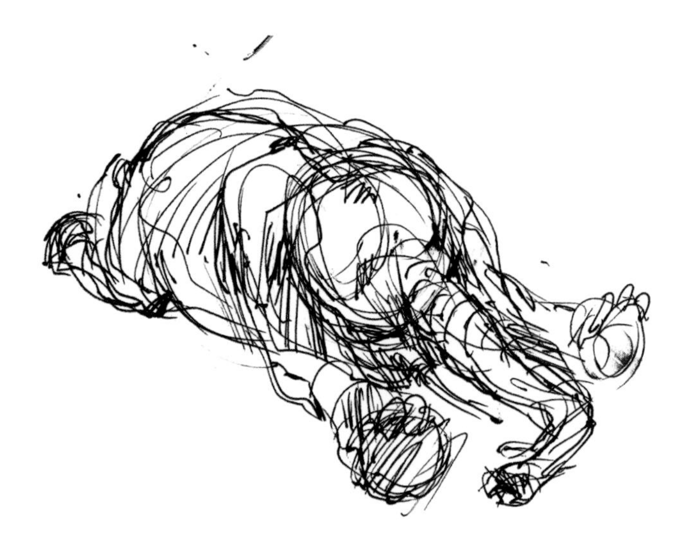

The case began on September 25, 2005 and a decision was returned on December 20, 2005. Again, the Court ruled that the mandate to teach Intelligent Design was a violation of the US Constitution. Judge Jones wrote a 139 page decision which ruled that Intelligent Design was a religious belief, not an area of scientific discovery and research. On page 43 of the decision, Judge Jones wrote the following, "The overwhelming evidence at trial established that Intelligent Design is a religious view, a mere re-labeling of creationism, and not a scientific theory."

The eight Dover School Board members who supported intelligent design's inclusion in the science curriculum were defeated in a November 8, 2005 election. The new members of the school board, who opposed the teaching of intelligent design in science classes, said they would not appeal Judge Jones' decision.

The Kansas State School Board also engaged in the Intelligent Design/Evolution battle. In May 2005, the Kansas State Board held hearing on the scientific merit of evolution and then adopted new science standards that were called the Critical Analysis of Evolution. On August 1, 2006, 4 of the 6 Republicans who supported the new standards regarding evolution lost their re-election campaigns. In 2007, the Kansas State School Board switched back to the science standards.

WHO NEEDS A CRUISE SHIP WHEN WE CAN VACATION ON THE ARK

Since the Creationism crew could not win in the courtroom or classroom they had to find another arena to enter. Their next logical step was...tourism! Perhaps the proposed Bibleland USA Christian Theme Park in Tennessee is a bit too much fun for the Creationism crowd. On May 28, 2007, Memorial Day, The Answers in Genesis Ministry opened the $27 million Creation Museum. The 60,000 square foot museum located in Northern Kentucky, just outside of Cincinnati, attempts to explain everything.

Among the things you can learn in the Museum is that dinosaurs and humans hung out in peace in the Garden of Eden before Eve picked that apple. Dinosaurs were also on the ark with Noah. Just so you can relive the experience, there is a full scale replica of the Ark in the Museum. The Museum even has a planetarium and a special effects theatre with vibrating seats. The Museum also has a gift shop and a restaurant will serve no animal older than 6,000 years old.

So, if you don't like what Junior is getting in the classroom, spend the $20 (only $10 for the kiddies) and get them re-educated. You can also buy an annual pass for $60 because it is hard to see all 6,000 years in one visit. You probably won't be alone; the museum had over 100,000 visitors in its first two months and is predicting 250,000 visitors in its first year.

Growth Through Mass Extinction
pen, ink, acrylic
2006

For any creature to evolve, the top of the food chain must parish. Small mammals lived with the dinosaurs during the Cretaceous Period (not Jesus) and remained that size. They couldn't evolve into larger animals due to the dinosaur's dominance over the food chain. Once there was a global catastrophe, the food source for the dinosaurs disappeared and they could no longer survive. The mammals being much smaller, needed less food to sustain themselves and this gave them a chance to evolve into what we are today.

BUT ISN'T EVOLUTION JUST A THEORY?

The phrase 'Scientific Theory' does not carry the same meaning as 'theory' in everyday life. Paleontologist Stephen Jay Gould explains: "Evolution is a theory. It is also a fact. And facts and theories are different things, not rungs in a hierarchy of increasing certainty. Facts are the world's data. Theories are structures of ideas that explain and interpret facts. Facts do not go away when scientists debate rival theories to explain them. Einstein's theory of gravitation replaced Newton's, but apples did not suspend themselves in mid-air, pending the outcome. And humans evolved from ape-like ancestors whether they did so by Darwin's proposed mechanism or by some other yet to be discovered."

WHAT IS THE REAL LESSON TO BE LEARNED?

The Bible's creation story is contained in Genesis chapters 1–3. In these three chapters, God created the world and everything in it and leaves man in charge. God says stay away from the apple but not too long after that Adam and Eve mess everything up.

There are three central elements to the creation story in Genesis. 1. God values human life more than anything else. 2. God made the world beautiful—and that beauty remains. 3. Mankind, when given the opportunity to be obedient to God, screws things up.

Human beings, in spite of having a special place in God's creation, have been disobedient from the beginning. The rest of the Old Testament is about God working with the sons of Abraham to restore that relationship through Israel. And the plot line of the New Testament is about God giving his Son so that all mankind can have their relationship with God restored. The rest of the Bible from the fourth chapter of Genesis on is about God's attempts to woo us back and mankind being a bunch of boneheads.

What happened 6,000 years ago (Creationism) or 4.5 billion years ago (Evolution) does not remove the reality of today. Nor should it be an excuse for further disobedience from God. If God made us and the earth—yet we continue to do battle with both—how faithful are we? Again, if the shepherds of the Religious Right can keep their sheep busy with 'where we came from' debate, then perhaps the flock will be less concerned with where we are going as a nation and a world.

William Jennings Bryan once said, "All the ills from which America suffers can be traced to the teaching of evolution." There are ample ways to disagree with this line of reasoning but one of the ways is to attack the hopelessness and apathy in Bryan's words. Much can be done today to make things better for all. Bryan's words serve as an excuse to do nothing but player-hate.

Get Your Evolution On pen, ink, acrylic, 2006

More drawings from the Cleveland Museum of Natural History. In this piece is an extinct Republican Creationist skull. Title is taken from a song by Clutch.

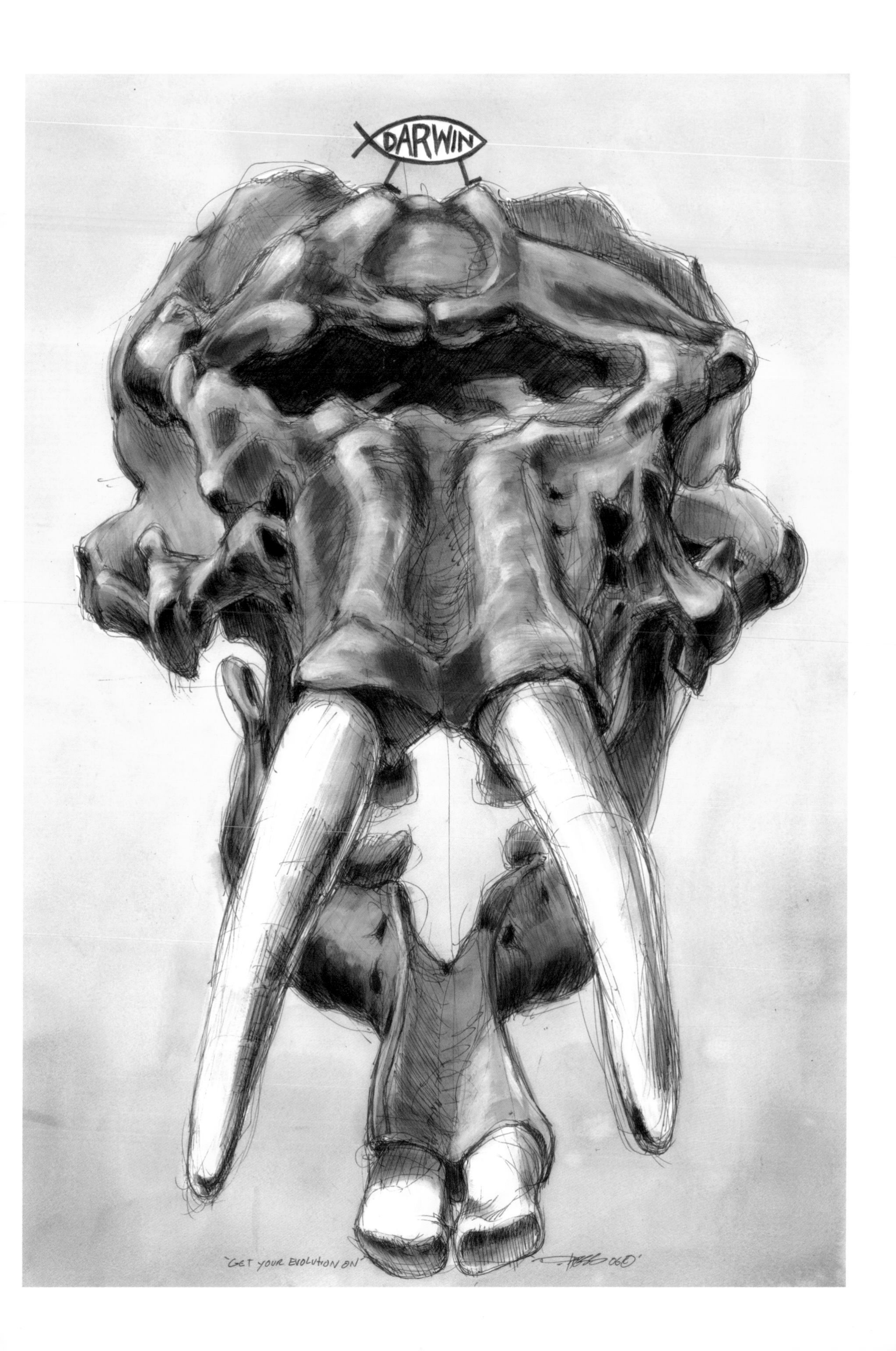
DARWIN
"GET YOUR EVOLUTION ON"

'FICTION AND CHIPS'

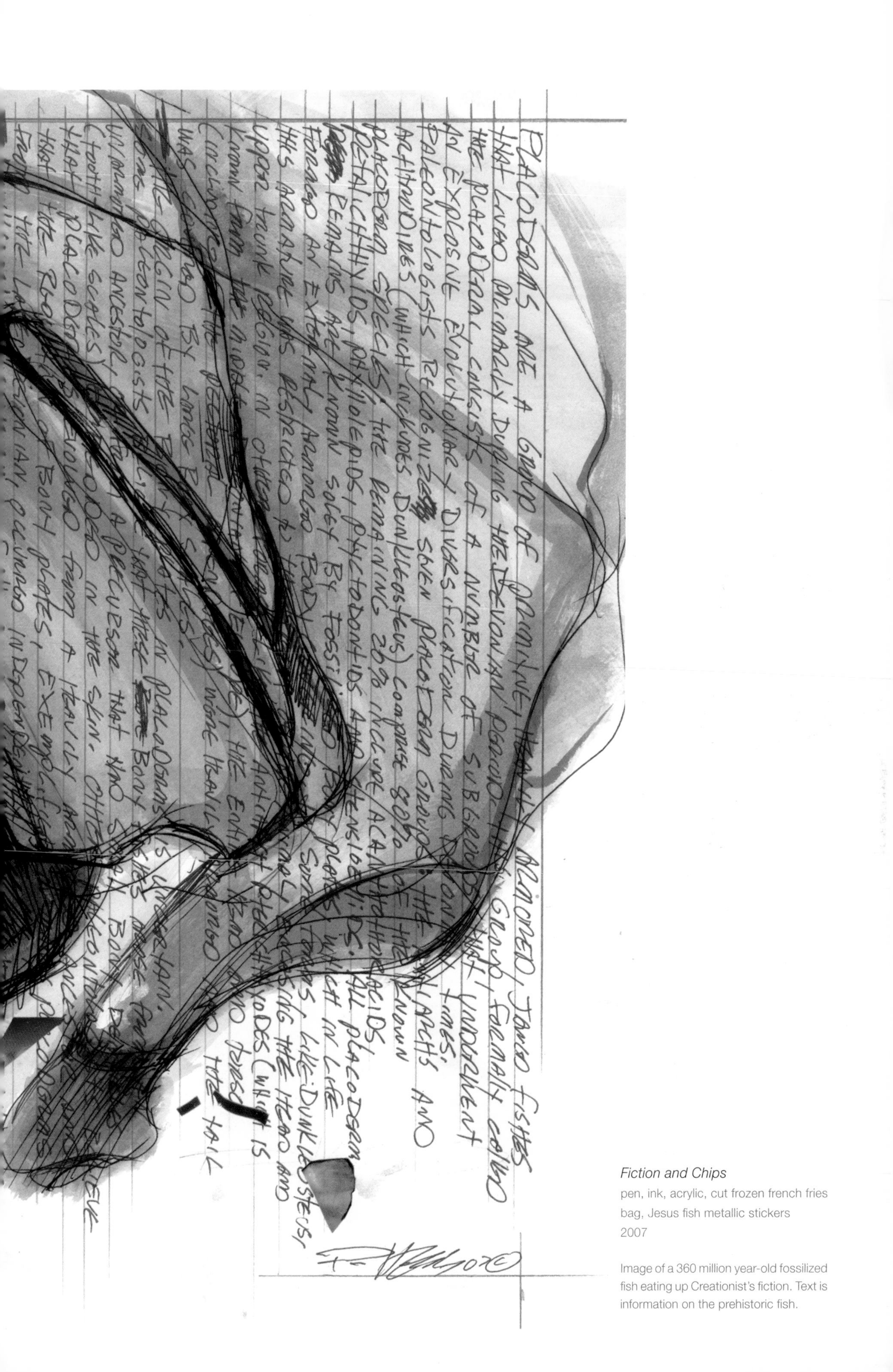

Fiction and Chips
pen, ink, acrylic, cut frozen french fries bag, Jesus fish metallic stickers
2007

Image of a 360 million year-old fossilized fish eating up Creationist's fiction. Text is information on the prehistoric fish.

Cave Men Look Like Jesus

pen, ink, acrylic

2007

Evolve
pen, ink, acrylic
2006

THE RED ELEPHANT TRAMPLES STEM CELLS

On July 19, 2006, President George Bush used the first veto of his presidency. In many ways, that was a pretty remarkable accomplishment. It demonstrated how long the Republican controlled Congress and the Republican President were in lock-step together. Remember when Bush won the election by a 5–4 vote of the US Supreme Court, the Republicans controlled Congress? The Democrats did not regain control of Congress until after November 2006, so this veto must have been significant because it was the first time Bush and the majority of Congress disagreed. The issue that created the historic rift was the use of federal dollars for stem cell research. Even Tennessee Republican Senator (and surgeon) Bill Frist supported the restoration of federal stem cell funding. (Bush would veto Stem Cell research again on June 20, 2007, after the Democrats took control of Congress.)

We have examined the decisions made by this administration. Their priorities are: 1. Can we make money from it somehow (the 'More for Me' Plan)? 2. Should we play to our Religious Right base (the Abortion issue)? 3. If scientists are behind it then it has gotta be bad (Global Warming & Clean Energy).

The majority of Americans support stem cell research. Maybe George Bush would allow stem cell research if Halliburton could make money from it?

STEM CELL BACKGROUND

Embryonic Stem Cells are a form of infertility treatment in which the fertilization of sperm and egg is induced in a laboratory setting. These embryos are either implanted in a woman's uterus or when not used—destroyed. These embryos are smaller than this "." They are less than the size of a grammatical period. The controversy centers on whether there is another use for the unused embryos.

Scientists are eager to unlock the mysteries of stem cells. By their very nature, stem cells can develop into any kind of human cell. Embryonic stem cells can morph into any of the 220 types of human cells that become human tissue. Stem cells could be better than duct tape; able to change into and repair many essential human organs.

Paralyzed rats have had their spinal cords heal when they were injected with stem cells. Research like this provides hope all across the medical community. That is why so many with all sorts of debilitating diseases (not just paralysis, but also cancer, muscular dystrophy, or Parkinson's disease) are advocating for research in this emerging field of knowledge. Who knows what discoveries will be found in the next petri dish?

Scientists were first able to conduct experiments on embryonic stem cells in 1998. On August 9, 2001, President Bush said that federal research could only be used on stem cells already in use. He banned the use of federal funding on all stem cell research from that point forward. One of the consequences of this decision is that leading stem cell scientists are now practicing their craft in other nations including Great Britain, Singapore and Taiwan.

Steaming From The Right-eous

pen, ink, acrylic

2006

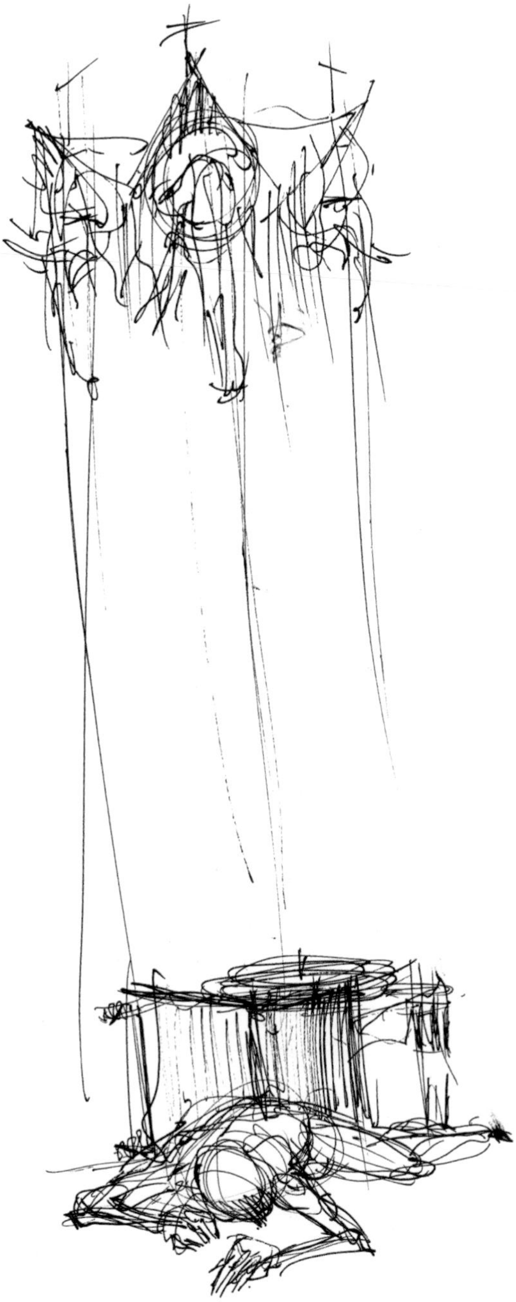

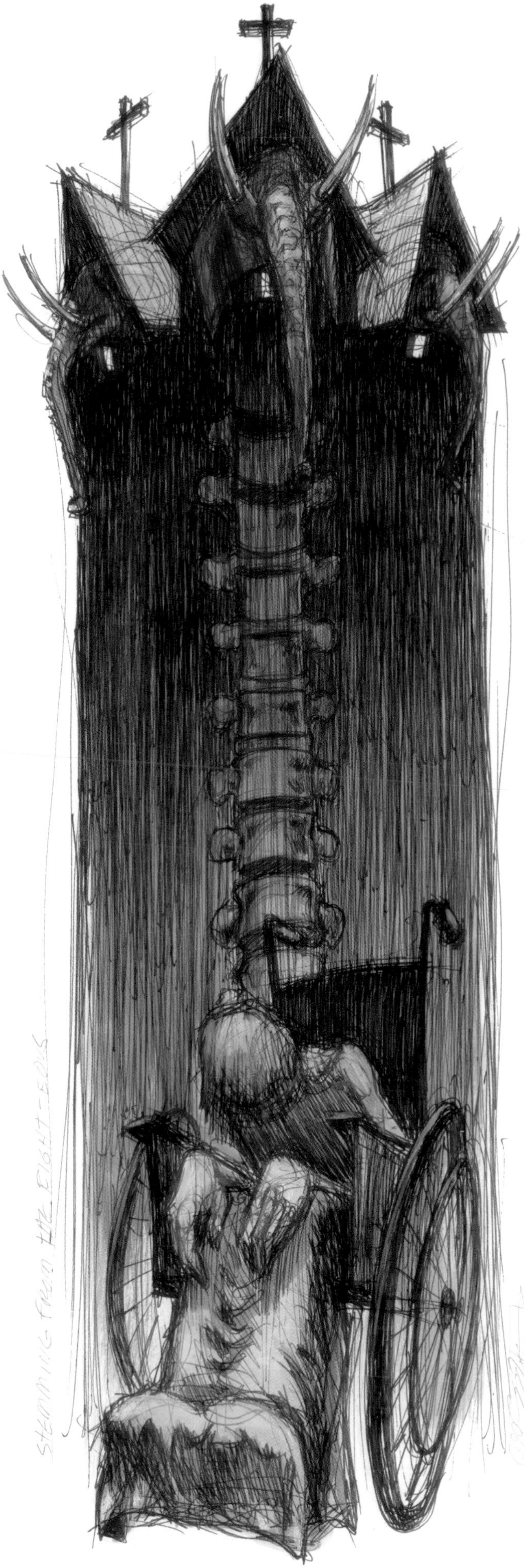

I wanted to create the feeling of oppression from both the church and state in this one. At eye level, I have the figure in the wheel chair hunched over implying weight. Behind him I drew the spine that leads your eye up to the church towers, which are doing what towers do, towering. Lurking within the steeples are the red elephants, raising the question, are the Republicans doing the church's bidding, or is the church doing the Republican's bidding? Do either of them know at this point?

WHAT IS THE STEM CELL CONTROVERSY?

The stem cell debate centers on the ethics of using embryonic stem cells for research purposes when those embryos could develop into human life. The President has said, "Destroying human life in the hopes of saving human life is not ethical." This fits nicely with the anti-abortion arguments the Religious Right has grown accustomed to hearing from the GOP. But as mentioned in the very first paragraph, this issue must somehow be different. Remember, it attracted enough Republican support to create the need for Bush's first ever veto. When asked why Bush was opposed to the federal stem cell funding, White House spokesman Tony Snow said on July 18, 2006, "The simple answer is he thinks murder is wrong." Good thing the White House is not overreacting.

What the White House forgot is these frozen embryos will NOT become life unless they are planted into a female uterus. Also, if they are not surgically placed into a prospective human mother, they are destroyed. So is that murder—when unwanted medical waste is knowingly discarded? Why not use them for research? Why not use them to find cures? It is estimated that there are thousands of available embryos in fertility clinics across the country.

Christian teachings and beliefs often run counter to modern day science. Stem cells are not the first or final time the two will clash. It was once argued that anesthesia should not be used during childbirth because it was God's will for women to suffer during childbirth. Good thing that never caught on.

Yes, our scientific judgments need to be balanced with ethical discussions so we are not experimenting on humans like the Nazis did. No one is limiting the creation of life. No one is advocating the harvesting of embryos from unwilling mothers.

If you believe all human life is on the planet due to the hand of God, then you need to acknowledge that God gave human beings minds and the ability to reason. The process of logical inquiry called the scientific method is then a result of God's creation. Why limit the tools God has given us?

IT'S KINDA LIKE THIS

Here's an analogy. There once was a dam that broke on a river next to a collection of farms. Flood waters poured over the fields and destroyed crops, barns, and homes. Many of the farmers escaped harm; however, one farmer remained in his home. As flood waters rose he had to climb onto his roof.

This farmer was a religious man and was convinced God would save him. As he sat on his roof a boat came by and the rescuers pleaded with him to get into the boat so he could be taken to safety. He said, "no thanks." He told the boaters he believed God would rescue him. And the flood waters rose.

Soon a helicopter appeared overhead and the rescuers inside shouted down for the man to climb up a ladder they would drop down to him. He said thanks, but no thanks—he trusted God would rescue him. And the flood waters rose and the man drowned. When he stood before God he said, "Lord, I have always had great faith in your power and love, why then did you not rescue me from the flood?" And God said, "What are you talking about, I sent you a boat and a helicopter."

These frozen embryos, that will otherwise be discarded, may be sent from God to unlock the mysteries of yet uncured disease. Since August 9, 2001, George Bush has been waving off boats and helicopters that could have saved thousands.

SPONGEBOB AND SANTA
CARTOONS IN SHEEP'S CLOTHING

The 2004 election year had several interesting subplots, none more sinister than the removal of human rights by popular vote. Yes, it was a battle of Bush vs. Kerry, but in many states across the country the gay marriage issue was also before voters. There were anti-gay-marriage initiatives on the ballot in 11 states and the anti-gay side won every time.

This issue worked for the Bush campaign because it gave the Religious Right another reason to get out and vote. National exit polling indicated that 79% of anti-gay marriage voters also voted for Bush. Was the anti-gay issue the only reason W beat a Massachusetts liberal? No, but it certainly helped.

The big 11 state win led some of the leading conservative Christians to wonder what the next step would be. They saw the 2004 elections as a big step in restoring God's blessing to this sinful land. Now what could they do to keep the momentum moving? After defeating homosexuals the next logical step was to attack a cartoon character of course.

DOBSON OUTS A DRAWING

On January 19, 2005, Dr. James C. Dobson, founder of the influential conservative Christian organization, Focus On The Family, was speaking at a black tie dinner in Washington D.C. During his remarks, Dobson decided to show-off his knowledge of modern day culture when he suggested the cartoon character SpongeBob Squarepants was promoting homosexuality. SpongeBob was in a video with other cartoon characters that its creators claimed was designed to promote social tolerance. Dobson knew it really to promote homosexuality. The evidence that led Dobson to this conclusion was a scene where SpongeBob was holding hands with his friend Patrick. Patrick is a starfish. Do starfish even have hands?

Dr. Dobson is the most influential conservative Christian leader that you have never heard of. Dr. Dobson has a weekly newspaper column that runs in over 500 newspapers and has a nationally syndicated radio show. His Colorado Springs based organization receives so much mail it has its own zip code.

Dobson's cartoon character and starfish attack was not even original. He copied two prior gay attacks on children's characters. In 1994, Reverend Joseph Chambers attacked Sesame Street's Bert and Ernie as being gay because Bert taught Ernie how to sew. Not to be outdone, Jerry Falwell outed Teletubby, Tinky Winky for being gay friendly, if not an outright homosexual.

If you are straight and feeling a little left out, just let your memory drift back to one of the first attacks by the Religious Right on fictional characters. While he was serving as Vice President, Dan Quayle criticized fictional TV character Murphy Brown for having a child out of wedlock. Ahh, the good old days.

Since Santa and rock and roll are both under attack, I thought I'd combine the two by putting a KISS belt buckle on Santa. In the late 1970's, there was a rumor the letters K.I.S.S. was an anagram for "Knights In Satan's Service." Of course, KISS proved this to be true by putting out the song *I Was Made for Loving You* off of their *Dynasty* record. Nothing says evil like disco.

Funny
mixed media
2006

For this piece, I tweaked a popular chant used by the gay community. Instead of "we're here, we're queer, get used to it," I went with "we're here, we're cartoons, get used to it," to illustrate the Christian right's absurd notion that SpongeBob is gay. SpongeBob is a cartoon, people. He's not real...and even if he were gay, who cares? Each character was drawn and painted on small water color sketch book pages. I then mounted them on top of SpongeBob comic book pages. I used an acrylic transparent black wash over those comic pages which helps to knock down their brightness, keeping them from competing with the foreground drawings.

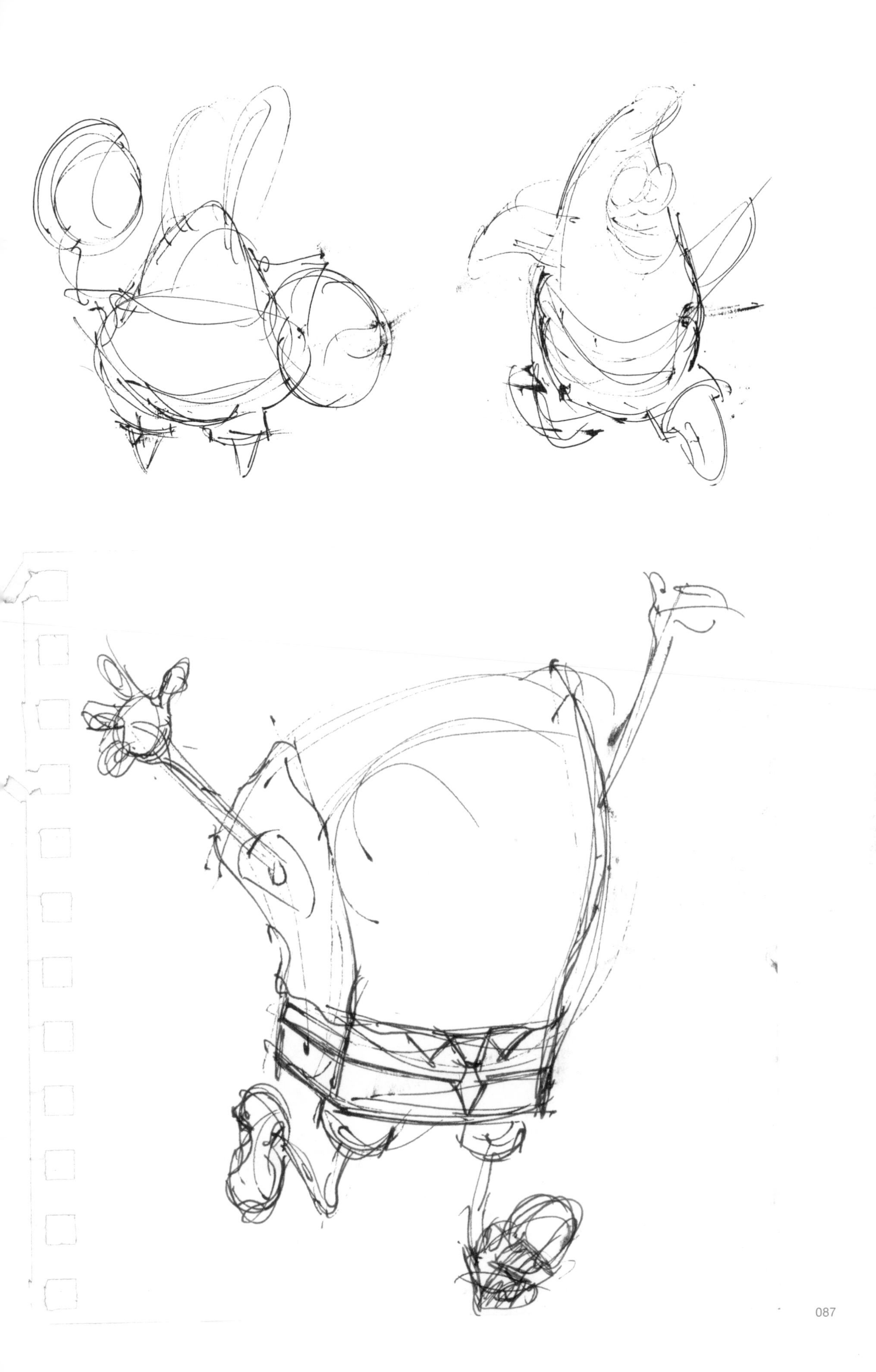

Knights In Satan's Service
pen and ink
2006

BAD SANTA

With Dobson on the attack against that sneaky and way too tolerant cartoon, Dial-the-Truth (DTT) Ministries in Alabama took on that other bastion of childhood happiness—Santa Claus. Yep, the guy who delivers gifts.

You can see why, can't you?! Let me spell out Dial-the-Truth's reasoning. If you want to check yourself, you can Google their website and order a copy of their anti-Santa literature entitled, "Santa Claus—the Great Imposter." We will see later why that title is more right than wrong, but first let's examine their reasons why we should fear Santa.

He might not even exist. They claim that Saint Nicholas' (Santa Claus' alias) existence is not attested by any historical document (no, I am not making this up). Santa seems to be an awful lot like the Norse god, Thor. After all, both Thor and Santa are elderly, white, male, friendly and kind of chubby. The topper...both have beards and both beards are WHITE! Read on—if you are not terrified.

Santa claims to have three God like qualities:

1. Santa claims to be all knowing or omniscient. Consider this well known statement, "He sees you when you are sleeping, he knows when you're awake. HE KNOWS IF YOU HAVE BEEN BAD OR GOOD."

2. Santa is everywhere or omnipresent. He is in the parades, he is at football games, he is at the mall and he is on TV. Santa is everywhere. He is like the domestic wiretapping program.

3. Santa is all powerful or omnipotent. He has the power to grant wishes.

Consider Santa's last name, "Nicholas." Adam Sandler was in a movie called "Little Nicky" in which Sandler played a character who was the son of Satan. Yup, you guessed it, "Nick" is a Satan name. No, this reason is not made up either.

But the topper is the following; by simply rearranging the letter "N" in Santa's name you can get Satan. Therefore Santa = Satan. Move the "N" and you change the wording, but not the meaning of either name because both Santa and Satan are the enemies of God.

the throne of his glory.
(Matthew 25:31)
Take a trip to the local mall at Christmas time. Go watch Santa sitting on his royal throne. Kids are lined up to sit on his lap of judgement. What does Santa ask them. "Have you been a good little boy?" "Have you been a good little girl?"
Millions of young children anxiously climb into the loving lap of their Santa. They will whisper into his ear their little hearts desire. Then they will jump out of bed Christmas morning, with eyes shimmering, and hearts pounding – and there is all the wonderful gifts Santa brought them.
Santa (or Satan. . . take your pick) has replaced God as the
giver of gifts and the one who answers their prayers.
to these kids at Christmas time. They just need to
Satan's ultimate goal – worship. He will offer you gifts – whomso-
ever I will I give it" – If thou therefore wilt worship me.
SANTA CLAUS: THE GREAT IMPOSTER
Copyright © 2005 Dr. Terry Watkins
Published by Dial-the-Truth Ministries

OUR DEFENSE OF SANTA

The first Dial-the-Truth claim: Did Saint Nicholas exist? Our answer—who cares? This is not to belittle anyone who is a relative of the actual Saint Nicholas or Saint Nicholas himself. It is just a really bad argument that Santa is a tool of Satan. That is like saying the reason why we invaded Iraq is because orange juice tastes so good. It just doesn't make any logical sense at all.

The second DTT claim: Are Santa and the Norse god, Thor the same dude? No. Yes, they are both fat guys who need a razor, but no one wants to say that because they are both friendly and good with the neighbor kids. But here is the real difference. Thor rides around on a chariot which is pulled by two goats. Whereas Santa has eight reindeer and they pull a sleigh; which, by the way, flies through the air.

There are some critical differences regarding how Santa and Thor ride. Many of these facts are difficult to dispute. OK maybe at a distance a goat could look like a reindeer and a chariot could look like a sleigh if they were both on the ground and the bottom was obscured. But how do you not know the difference between two goats and eight reindeer? And keep in mind, when Rudolph is hanging with Santa's transportation, then there are technically nine. And eight or nine are WAY more than two.

The third DTT claim: Yes, Santa does have some God-like features. Being able to deliver all those gifts does require super-human skills, but he is definitely not everywhere. He has yet to be seen at the car wash, water park or swimming pool. Maybe he does not swim all that well. Which again would be pretty clear evidence Santa is not God.

Untitled
mixed media
2006

There's a whole lot of mixed media going on in this piece. First off, I did the drawing of the Cub Scout sitting on the evil Santa's lap, finishing it with acrylic paint. When that was done, I burned the bottom edge of the page to suggest the fires of hell coming up from below. Next step was mounting this piece on top of Santa faced Christmas wrapping paper. After that was done, I incorporated clippings from Dial-the-Truth Ministry's flyer regarding the Santa and Satan debate. At this point, I felt the stark white paper from the Santa image and Dial-the-Truth flyer contrasted too much with the colorful wrapping paper. I needed to bring the two elements together as one. I decided a Santa face rubber stamper would do the trick. Starting with red acrylic paint followed by green, I stamped Santa's face around the border where the Santa drawing meets wrapping paper. This created a gradation between the two elements without flattening it out. Finally, to solidify this piece as one, a toothbrush dipped in acrylic paint was needed. By pulling my thumb across the bristles of the brush, I specked the top of the page with paint splatters making a second gradation, bringing together all the elements as one.

The fourth DTT claim is the horrible movie *Little Nicky* demonstrates that Satan often goes by the name Nicholas, just like Saint Nicholas. The greatest thing about this claim is it means somebody at Dial-the-Truth Ministries went to see *Little Nicky.* Nobody saw that movie. The Dial-the-Truth people should have stayed at home and watched basic cable. Anyone who knows anything about Satan knows that he is Saddam Hussein's love interest on the *South Park* TV Show. And Adam Sandler is not even on that show.

The fifth and final claim is if you change the letters around of Santa—you get Satan. Brilliant. Now let's try the same anagram test with Dial-the-Truth Ministries. If you rearrange the letters of Dial-the-Truth you can also get "Adult Thither." Hmmmm, maybe they are just after money. Perhaps that would explain why they are selling the tract "Santa Claus—the Great Imposter" on their website. Maybe they are just fanning the flames of Christian panic to sell stuff and make a buck. Let's see if there are any hidden meanings behind the letters that create "Ministries"? Oh wait, no need to worry, unless you think the phrase "I'm Sinister" is nothing to worry about. Another meaning could be "Tim is Risen", but we don't know who Tim is, so it has to be the Sinister thing. The anagram test proves it. The Dial-the-Truth attack on Santa Claus is just a sinister plan to take money from gullible believers.

Here is a special message to the faithful at Dial-the-Truth Ministries, Santa is a myth; folklore if you will. The biggest reason Santa is "The Great Imposter" is he was never alive. He is a fictional character, much like SpongeBob—he does not exist. The evidence you use to make your case against Santa include an Adam Sandler movie, which is also fiction.

When you go to a play and someone dies on stage, do you believe they are really dead? Oftentimes, the same character is brought back to life for the very next performance. How does that happen? Can resurrections be that commonplace? When you are in a movie theatre and there is a shoot out, how come no one who is sitting in the theatre gets wounded? Do something worthwhile and open a soup kitchen somewhere. Or do you not believe in poverty or soup?

FYI: In later chapters, we shall hear again from Dial-the-Truth Ministries.

MAKE UP YOUR MIND—IS FICTION GOOD OR BAD?

It is good to know the same group who relied upon fictional WMD evidence to sacrifice 4,000 American lives also attacks fictional characters. To be a faithful member of the Red Elephant Crew you need to ignore facts (stem cell, global warming) and make your decisions based upon fiction (The Iraq War & SpongeBob). If nothing else, there is a consistency in their madness.

The Devil Is In The Chimney
pen, ink, acrylic, flyer and comic book clippings
2006

Satan comes from the fires of Hell, and Santa comes from the fires of the place, both are coming from a source of fire. This coincidence along with moving the letters around in their names (moving Santa's "N" to the end of his name = Satan), is proof positive that Santa is in league with the Devil. On the mantel, I mounted a clipping from a 1969 comic book ad for Christmas Seals. I thought the image of the little girl kissing Santa was too cool not to incorporate into this piece.

The Devil is in the Chimney
The fact is that Santa and Satan are alter egos, brothers; they have the same origin... On the surface, the two figures are polar opposites, but underneath they share the same parent, and both retain many of the old symbols associated with their "father"... From these two paths, he arrived at both the warmth of our fireplace and in the flames of hell.
DIAL-THE-TRUTH
MINISTRIES
5990 Willow Ridge Road
Pinson, AL 35126 • (205) 681-9956
www.av1611.org
Recorded message at (205) 680-9206

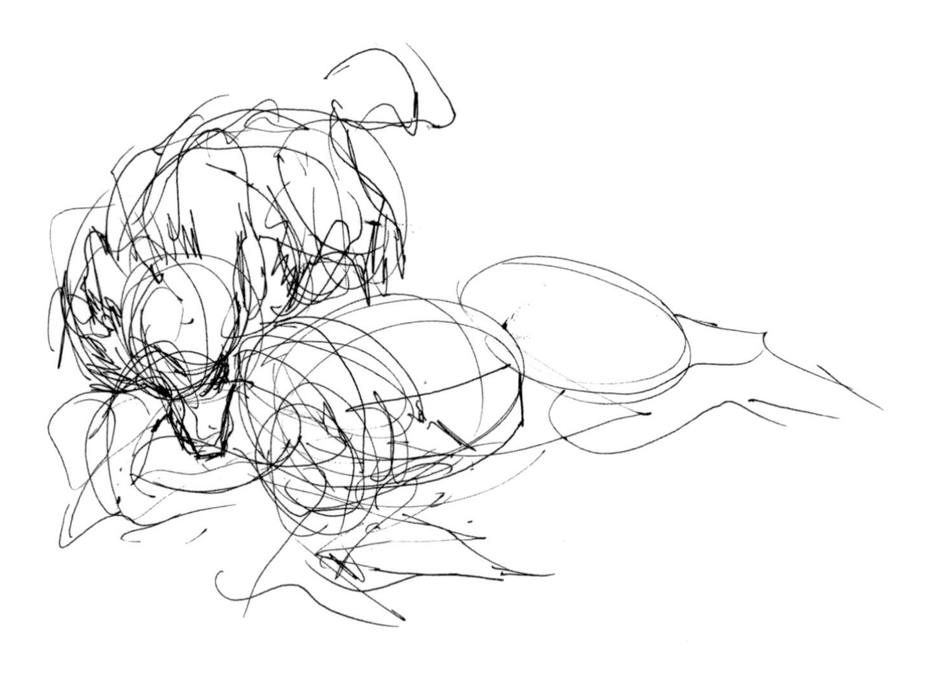

JOSÉ: MEDIA WATCH DOG

ALL THE NEWS THAT FITS

In *Good Dog...or Jihad on the American Aljazeera,* José (Derek's dog) has taken down a Fox. You can tell its a fox because it says so on the tummy.

"FREEDOM OF THE PRESS IS LIMITED TO THOSE WHO OWN ONE." –**A.J. LIEBBLING, AMERICAN JOURNALIST**

"JOURNALISTS MUST SEEK AND SPEAK THE TRUTH, FOR WE ARE THE VOICE OF THE VOICELESS MILLIONS."
–**RAZIA BHATT, PAKISTANI JOURNALIST**

HOW FAKE NEWS HAPPENS—CONSIDER TWO EXAMPLES

In May 2003, *The New York Times* reporter, Jayson Blair was found to have plagiarized the details of a story from another newspaper. An internal investigation eventually discovered that he had fabricated details in 36 of 73 stories that he wrote for *The New York Times* including one about the West Virginia home life of Iraqi War hostage Jessica Lynch. Blair and later two of his supervisors resigned.

On April 1, 2006 the highly respected *British Medical Journal* published an article about a new scientific discovery by Australian scientists that identified a motivation deficiency disorder that they named MoDeD. The scientist had concluded that extreme laziness could be a result of a medical condition. The story was false, it was made up as an April Fool's Day joke. But, the interview requests came flying in and a few news organizations ran the story before discovering the joke.

The good news is that these falsehoods were unique. One was discovered and one was just a prank. But, what if falsehoods are not a fluke, but are instead, company policy?

SO WHO WOULD WANT TO CONTROL THE NEWS?

There is a dangerous assumption in America that the free press in a free country is free of opinions. Especially when one of the major networks is run by a former Republican media strategist. Ladies and gentleman, meet Roger Ailes, the President of the Fox News Channel. Ailes is a former media strategist who worked for Republican Presidents Nixon, Reagan and the first George Bush. Ailes worked alongside Lee Atwater in crafting the media strategies that George Bush used against Michael Dukakis in the 1988 elections. Does anyone remember the controversial Willie Horton ads? Do you think Mr. Ailes has a partisan agenda, or do you think he is just an honest news guy?

CAN FAIR AND BALANCED BE FACTUAL AND ACCURATE?

An October 2003 study by the University of Maryland's Program on International Policy Attitudes (PIPA) revealed many misperceptions held by Americans about the Iraq War. But, the study went beyond naming the misinformation, it attempted to trace the source of the incorrect viewpoints.

PIPA conducted seven polls between January and September of 2003 and it discovered that the number of misperceptions held by Americans varied greatly with their choice of primary news source. It also affected the degree of support for the war. The more inaccuracies that were held by individuals, the higher their personal support of the Iraq War.

The results revealed that if you were watching Fox News you were more likely to believe something that was not true. The "best" media source for educating its viewers/listeners, according to the survey, was NPR and PBS. For example, the belief that Weapons of Mass Destruction were found in Iraq was held by 33% of Fox News viewers whereas only 11% of NPR/PBS viewers believed that misperception.

Another stat, the belief that Saddam Hussein's Iraqi government had a link with Al Qaeda was held by 67% of Fox News viewers where as only 16% of NPR/PBS viewers held that false viewpoint.

If the goal is spreading propaganda, then Fox News is working. If the goal is getting the correct information to the public so that they can make well informed decisions, then America might have better luck with Dial-the-Truth Ministries.

The PIPA study may have been one of the reasons why Bush has attempted to weaken public broadcasting. After all, if you don't like the message, you can always attack the messenger. These attacks came two ways—Bush appointed Republican political hacks and a proposal to substantially cut the budget.

He has appointed a series of Republican Party loyalists to the board of the Corporation for Public Broadcasting (CPB), the body that runs PBS. In October of 2005, Chairman Ken Tomlinson (a Bush appointee) resigned when an internal CPB report came out, which accused Tomlinson of attempting to impose a Right leaning partisan agenda on PBS programming.

Other Bush appointees to the CPB board include Cheryl Halpern and Gay Hart Gaines, both of whom have donated large sums of money to Republican causes and candidates.

If Bush's new board members cannot soften up the programming he will just make it harder to operate. In February 2007, Bush proposed a 25% budget cut to the federal support of PBS funding.

OUR CHALLENGE AS INFORMATION CONSUMERS

One of the greatest things about this nation is the unfettered access to political discourse and opinion. But, there is danger within that freedom—that we become apathetic in what we feed our minds. Too often, the news is a 'he said-she said' exchange of party line BS with no pursuit of the truth. The reader does not become wiser because the story contained empty bravado. Yes, the press needs to be objective and present both sides, but it also needs to analyze the facts and shine its light in dark corners and look for the truth.

On May 15, 2005, with PBS under assault by the Bush administration, Bill Moyers delivered a stirring defense of the press at the National Conference for Media Reform. Among the highlights of the Moyers address were:

"AN UNCONSCIOUS PEOPLE, AN INDOCTRINATED PEOPLE, A PEOPLE FED ONLY ON PARTISAN INFORMATION AND OPINION THAT CONFIRM THEIR OWN BIAS, A PEOPLE MADE MORBIDLY OBESE IN MIND AND SPIRIT BY THE JUNK FOOD OF PROPAGANDA, IS LESS INCLINED TO PUT UP A FIGHT, TO ASK QUESTIONS AND BE SKEPTICAL. THAT KIND OF ORTHODOXY CAN KILL A DEMOCRACY."

"THESE 'RULES OF THE GAME' PERMIT WASHINGTON OFFICIALS TO SET THE AGENDA FOR JOURNALISM, LEAVING THE PRESS ALL TOO OFTEN SIMPLY TO RECOUNT WHAT OFFICIALS SAY INSTEAD OF SUBJECTING THEIR WORDS AND DEEDS TO CRITICAL SCRUTINY. INSTEAD OF ACTING AS FILTERS FOR READERS AND VIEWERS, SIFTING THE TRUTH FROM THE PROPAGANDA, REPORTERS AND ANCHORS ATTENTIVELY TRANSCRIBE BOTH SIDES OF THE SPIN INVARIABLY FAILING TO PROVIDE CONTEXT, BACKGROUND OR ANY SENSE OF WHICH CLAIMS HOLD UP AND WHICH ARE MISLEADING."

"I ALWAYS THOUGHT THE AMERICAN EAGLE NEEDED A LEFT WING AND A RIGHT WING. THE RIGHT WING WOULD SEE TO IT THAT ECONOMIC INTERESTS HAD THEIR LEGITIMATE CONCERNS ADDRESSED. THE LEFT WING WOULD SEE TO IT THAT ORDINARY PEOPLE WERE INCLUDED IN THE BARGAIN. BOTH WOULD KEEP THE GREAT BIRD ON COURSE. BUT WITH TWO RIGHT WINGS OR TWO LEFT WINGS, IT'S NO LONGER AN EAGLE AND IT'S GOING TO CRASH."

IN HIS SPEECH, MOYERS QUOTED HISTORIAN RICHARD REEVES WHO SAID, "REAL NEWS IS THE NEWS THAT HELPS YOU AND I KEEP OUR FREEDOMS."

Good Dog....or Jihad On The American Aljazeera pen, ink, acrylic, 2006

That's my boy José with his righteous kill. Dogs can sense evil.

'CAN ALJAZEERAH"

ROCK AND ROLL AIN'T NOISE POLLUTION

"THINK FOR YOURSELF AND LET OTHERS ENJOY THE PRIVILEGE TO DO SO, TOO." – VOLTAIRE

THE INSPIRATION BEHIND THE ART. COULD IT BE...SATAN OR IS IT ADULT THITHER?

One of the major focal points of the December 15 art show was a rock and roll inspired section. But, it was not just rock and roll, it was also the Dial-the-Truth Ministries (excuse me, Adult Thither, I'm Sinister) attack on rock and roll artists. After Dial-the-Truth finished bringing Santa down to size they decided to go after works of poetry set to music and popular with the youth of today.

Adult Thither, I'm Sinister created another Christian tract called *The Devil's Advocate* which Hess incorporated into artwork. The basic premise of the tract is if your kids are listening to popular music then hide the knives because they are about to go on a rock and roll inspired, Devil possessed, killing spree. The tract highlights most of the anticipated offenders, Metallica, KISS, Marilyn Manson, Led Zeppelin, Slayer, Black Sabbath, Ozzy Osborne, Iron Maiden, AC/DC, Mötley Crüe, and Megadeath. It seems after they saw the movie *Little Nicky*, they went home to watch Headbangers Ball on MTV.

But they also outed Bow Wow Wow, Jimmy Buffet and Rod Stewart as tools of Santa or Satan. Derek Hess created four works of art of musicians and bands which had been targeted by Adult Thither, I'm Sinister; including Jimmy Buffet (that devilish Parrothead) and Rod Stewart. These are all very strong pieces of art, but to understand the Rod Stewart piece you really need to see the tract. The scholars at Adult Thither have confused Rod Stewart with Sid Vicious and the rest of the Sex Pistols. They source the song *Anarchy in the U.K.* as having been recorded by Rod Stewart. Brilliant. So, the artwork is Rod Stewart's physical features in Sid Vicious' wardrobe.

The Dial-the-Truth website also features other evidence that rock and roll music is a tool of the Devil including the premature death of rock stars. They document the natural and unnatural death of rock stars and the age of their demise. 321 rockers have passed away early and their average age was 36.9 years old. Rock solid proof that being a minstrel for the Devil is bad for your health. Mind you, Adult Thither does not try to explain how in the world Keith Richards has lasted so long.

The real reason kids today are listening to dark, depressing music is they just found out that Santa is one of the Devil's loyal soldiers if not Satan himself. No wonder they are listening to *Cheeseburger in Paradise*.

KIDS TODAY

"I SEE NO HOPE FOR THE FUTURE OF OUR PEOPLE IF THEY ARE DEPENDENT ON THE FRIVOLOUS YOUTHS OF TODAY, FOR CERTAINLY ALL YOUTH ARE RECKLESS BEYOND WORDS. WHEN I WAS A BOY, WE WERE TAUGHT TO BE DISCRETE AND RESPECTFUL OF ELDERS, BUT THE PRESENT YOUTH ARE EXCEEDINGLY WISE AND IMPATIENT OF RESTRAINT." **-HESIOD, GREEK POET, 700 BC**

It seems like today's youth have been going to hell in a hand basket for generations, if not centuries. The kids next door to Hesiod must have had a pool party or something. Chances are if Hesiod were alive today, he would be a tract writer for Dial-the-Truth.

Sid Stewart

pen, ink, acrylic, flyer clippings, safety pin

2006

This one is priceless…Dial-the-Truth Ministries quotes, "I am an anti-christ" from the landmark record, *Anarchy In The U.K.* by Rod Stewart …well Rod can loosen up a pretty French gown, but he couldn't fan the flames of the late 1970's punk rock…as anyone who's graduated "Punk 101" knows, *Anarchy In The U.K.* is by the Sex Pistols. So, the name from this piece comes from the union of Sid Vicious and Rod Stewart.

Untitled
pen, ink, acrylic, flyer clipping
2006

Sixteen-year-old, Dennis Bartts, of Center Point, Texas, told his best friend he "planned to meet Satan." He walked to the high school football field, carrying his portable cassette player. When he got there he popped AC/DC's "Highway to Hell" in the cassette player, and hung himself from the goalpost.

CULTURE VERSUS CENSORSHIP—GUESS WHO ALWAYS WINS?

Censorship works best in dictatorships. When the government controls everything, then keeping the news in line is just a part of the package. However, censorship does not work as well in capitalistic nations where freedom of speech exists. In the marketplace of ideas, people vote with their dollars.

I BELIEVE IN CENSORSHIP. I MADE A FORTUNE OUT OF IT." –MAE WEST

According to Ms. West, unless you are going to remove major sections of the Constitution, censorship will most likely cause short-term sales spikes which might launch rock and roll legends.

The following artists and songs have been banned or censored: The Rolling Stones, *I Can't Get No Satisfaction*; Van Morrison, *Brown Eyed Girl*; The Doors, *Light My Fire*; Rod Stewart, *Tonight's the Night*; Peter Paul and Mary, *Puff the Magic Dragon*; and Olivia Newton John, *Physical*.

The most famous conflict in the music vs. government censorship fight was the Parents Music Resource Center (PMRC) hearings in the US Senate. The PMRC was founded by Tipper Gore, Susan Baker and 20 other Washington wives in May 1985 after Tipper heard *Darling Nikki* by Prince coming from her 12 year-old daughter's bedroom radio. Mrs. Gore realized this was not a passing song on the radio, but that she had purchased the album for her daughter.

The PMRC Congressional Hearings were held in the US Senate chambers on September 19, 1985. The PMRC wanted music lyrics printed on the outside of album covers. Music deemed to be too controversial would not be out on the sales racks, but rather would be sold from behind the counter. Yes, parental warning labels were eventually put on album covers in 1990, but (in the words of cartoon character Bart Simpson) that just helped the kids decide what to buy when they went shopping.

The PMRC also identified fifteen musical artists that were especially offensive, dubbed the filthy fifteen. They included AC/DC, Black Sabbath, Cyndi Lauper, Def Leppard, Judas Priest, Madonna, Mary Jane Girls, Mercyful Fate, Mötley Crüe, Prince, Sheena Easton, Twisted Sister, Vanity, Venom and W.A.S.P. Again, consider the wisdom of Mae West and the shopping tips of Bart Simpson. Was the goal of censorship good or bad for the majority of those musical artists?

Testifying on behalf of musicians was John Denver, Frank Zappa and Dee Snider. The music won. Frank Zappa said the following before US Senators, "It is my understanding that in law, First Amendment issues are decided with a preference for the least restrictive alternative. In this context, the PMRC demands are the equivalent of treating dandruff by decapitation."

THEN WHY DO THEY DO IT?

So why would a government, in a free country, attack modern day culture such as music, film or art? Because the political benefits outweigh the political risks. And why is that? Because young people do not vote.

How does the government know this? Because your birthday is a part of your voter registration record. They know how many 18–30-year-olds are registered to vote and they know how many actually punch a ballot on Election Day.

Let me explain. Voters are identified by age and address. If every person who is smart and beautiful and 25 went to the polls, then government policy would be more attentive to the needs of the smart and beautiful 25-year-olds.

So, if you are a young mom and need better child care options in your town…vote. If you have to work to pay for college… vote. If you want economic policies that support living wage jobs…vote. If you want your government to develop programs that can build towards a better future for this country…VOTE. And yes, if you want to stop censorship…vote. There is power not just in your one vote, but in segments of the population expressing their collective interest in all future public policies. If you want more government to pay attention to you then you need to be heard.

"ONE OF THE PENALTIES FOR REFUSING TO PARTICIPATE IN POLITICS IS THAT YOU END UP BEING GOVERNED BY YOUR INFERIORS.
–PLATO, ANCIENT GREEK PHILOSOPHER , 428 B.C.–348 B.C.

Plato was much cooler than Hesiod.

ROCK AND ROLL SAVES THE WORLD

It also might be important to point out that occasionally the minstrels of Satan's music box do some good. On July 13, 1985, a group of musicians came together for a concert in Philadelphia and in London. The concert was called Live Aid and its goal was to raise one million pounds (about $1.6 million) for starvation relief in Africa. The event featured many of the leading acts of the day. The concert was broadcast into more than 100 countries and was seen by an estimated 1.5 billion viewers. It raised over $280 million.

Untitled pen, ink, acrylic, flyer clipping, 2006

In this piece I thought the AC/DC lightening bolt from their logo would work well coming out of a rain cloud. The bottom edge is burnt to represent the fires of hell.

FORGET THE CHECK
WE'LL GET
HELL TO PAY
R HESS
11-30-80

AC/DC drawing
1980

This drawing of AC/DC is from one of my high school sketchbooks. Young artists tend to draw what they're interested in. For myself, I've always been inspired by rock music and lyrical content. This particular drawing was done shortly after the release of the landmark AC/DC record *Back In Black*. *Back In Black* was the first record of theirs to come out after the death of AC/DC's original singer Bon Scott. In February 1980, Bon passed out in his car after a night of heavy drinking and choked to death on his own vomit. One of the songs on *Back In Black* is titled "Have A Drink On Me." And one of the lines from the song is "forget the check, we'll get hell to pay." In my drawing there's an upside down pentagram with those lyrics written on it. Behind the pentagram is Bon Scott and the Devil watching the band play on from the other side, which in this case is hell. Now, I was inspired by this song, and many other heavy metal songs of the time, but I didn't grow up to worship Satan, or sacrifice goats. I guess Dial-the-Truth Ministries might be wrong some of the time.

GOOD THING THAT IS OVER

Or is it? After the 9/11 attacks, the largest radio station owner in America, Clear Channel Communications, decided to remove 166 lyrically questionable songs from its radio playlist. Those songs included:

AC/DC	*Dirty Deeds Done Dirt Cheap, Hells Bells, Highway to Hell*
Louis Armstrong	*What a Wonderful World*
The Bangles	*Walk Like an Egyptian*
The Beatles	*Lucy in the Sky with Diamonds, Ob-La-Di-Ob-La-Da*
Black Sabbath	*Sabbath Bloody Sabbath, War Pigs*
David Bowie & Mick Jagger	*Dancing in the Street*
Phil Collins	*In the Air Tonight*
The Cult	*Fire Woman*
Dave Matthews Band	*Crash into Me*
Deep Purple	*Smoke on the Water*
Neil Diamond	*America*
Celine Dion	*Love Can Move Mountains*
Gap Band	*You Dropped a Bomb on Me*
Norman Greenbaum	*Spirit in the Sky*
Billy Joel	*Only the Good Die Young*
Elton John	*Bennie and the Jets, Rocket Man*
Michael Jackson	*Beat It, Bad, Thriller*
Kansas	*Dust in the Wind*
Carole King	*I Feel the Earth Move*
Led Zeppelin	*Stairway to Heaven*
John Lennon	*Imagine*
Jerry Lee Lewis	*Great Balls of Fire*
Bobby McFerrin	*Don't Worry, Be Happy*
Don McLean	*American Pie*
Metallica	*Enter Sandman, Fade to Black, Seek & Destroy*
Steve Miller	*Jet Airliner*
Mitch Ryder & the Detroit Wheels	*Devil With a Blue Dress On*
Alanis Morissette	*Ironic*
Ricky Nelson	*Travelin' Man*
Nena	*99 Luftballons/99 Red Balloons*
Nine Inch Nails	*Head Like a Hole*
John Parr	*St. Elmo's Fire*
Peter, Paul and Mary	*Blowin' in the Wind, Leavin' on a Jet Plane*
Tom Petty	*Free Fallin'*
Pink Floyd	*Mother, Run Like Hell*
The Pretenders	*My City Was Gone*
Public Enemy	*911 Is a Joke*
Rage Against the Machine	*All Songs*
R.E.M.	*It's the End of the World as We Know It (And I Feel Fine)*
Simon and Garfunkel	*Bridge Over Troubled Water*
Frank Sinatra	*New York, New York*
The Smashing Pumpkins	*Bullet With Butterfly Wings*
Soundgarden	*Black Hole Sun, Blow Up The Outside World, Fell on Black Days*
Bruce Springsteen	*I'm Goin' Down, I'm on Fire*
Edwin Starr/Bruce Springsteen	*War*
Steam	*Na Na Hey Hey Kiss Him Goodbye*
Cat Stevens	*Morning Has Broken, Peace Train*
Talking Heads	*Burning Down the House*
James Taylor	*Fire And Rain*
Temple of the Dog	*Say Hello 2 Heaven*
The Trammps	*Disco Inferno*
U2	*Sunday Bloody Sunday, Bullet the Blue Sky*
Van Halen	*Jump, Dancing in the Street*
The Youngbloods	*Get Together*

As tempting as it may be to listen less in a time of war and national testing, it is in America's best interest to hear more.

"WE ARE NOT AFRAID TO ENTRUST THE AMERICAN PEOPLE WITH UNPLEASANT FACTS, FOREIGN IDEAS, ALIEN PHILOSOPHIES, AND COMPETITIVE VALUES. FOR A NATION THAT IS AFRAID TO LET ITS PEOPLE JUDGE THE TRUTH AND FALSEHOOD IN AN OPEN MARKET IS A NATION THAT IS AFRAID OF ITS PEOPLE." –JOHN F. KENNEDY

Parrot Heads, You're Being Mislead
pen, ink, acrylic, flier clipping
2006

Now come on, I don't care for Jimmy Buffet either, but he is not evil. All Jimmy wants to do is party with his boater pals, eat cheeseburgers in paradise, and sell out large venues. Corrupting America's youth is the farthest thing from his mind...maybe corrupting America's baby boomers is more like it.

'DEICIDE'
06©

Deicide
pen, ink, acrylic
2006

OK, I'll give this one to Dial-the-Truth, *Deicide* is a tough one to defend (although, I have yet to kill anyone as a direct result from listening to *Deicide*.) This was just too fun of an idea not to draw. The 666 in the upside down cross hopscotch is seducing the young through innocent childhood games...step on a crack, break your momma's back.

There Is A God
mixed media
2006

ABOUT THE AUTHORS

DEREK HESS

From concert posters to politically charged fine art pieces, Cleveland-based artist Derek Hess has tested the waters of both the music and art world for over 15 years. Always a fan of music, Hess began creating promotional flyers for shows in Cleveland using his own unique vision and a play off the bands names and genre. These flyers soon garnered the attention of countless bands as well as both the Rock and Roll Hall of Fame and the Louvre in Paris, who both have Hess' art in their permanent collection.

In addition to posters for bands such as Pantera, Thursday, Pink Floyd and Pearl Jam, Hess has also created CD covers for bands like Sepultura, Unearth and MTV's Headbangers Ball. Hess has been featured in countless magazines including *Newsweek, Spin, Alternative Press* and *Juxtapoz* and television shows on networks including TLC, The Food Network, MTV, Fuse and VH1.

KENT SMITH

Kent Smith is an award winning Member of the Euclid Board of Education in Euclid, Ohio. He was first elected in 2001 and was re-elected in 2005. During his six years on the Euclid School Board, he has served as the Legislative Liaison and the School Board President. In 2006, Kent Smith became the local head of the Democratic Party, a position called the Euclid City Democratic Leader.

He has a Masters Degree in Urban Studies from Cleveland State University and is currently a Ph.D. candidate in the Economic Development program at Cleveland State. Kent Smith has worked as an Adjunct Researcher for Policy Matters Ohio and was a Contributing Writer for the Cleveland Free Times.

He can also make a pretty mean lasagna. His next book is anybody's guess.

Photo credit: Michael Parksv